D0728871

Henry David Aiken

BRANDEIS UNIVERSITY

Walter Kaufmann

PRINCETON UNIVERSITY

Michael Scriven

INDIANA UNIVERSITY

Abraham Edel

THE CITY COLLEGE OF THE
CITY UNIVERSITY OF NEW YORK

Peter A. Bertocci

BOSTON UNIVERSITY

Kenneth D. Benne

BOSTON UNIVERSITY

EDITED BY

George Barnett

MICHIGAN STATE UNIVERSITY

PHILOSOPHY

AND EDUCATIONAL

DEVELOPMENT

HOUGHTON MIFFLIN COMPANY · BOSTON

New York · Atlanta · Geneva, Ill. · Dallas · Palo Alto

Contents

FOREWORD   *vii*

EDITOR'S INTRODUCTION   *xi*

1. *Analytical Philosophy and Educational Development*
   Henry David Aiken, BRANDEIS UNIVERSITY   *1*

2. *Educational Development from the Point of View of a Normative Philosophy*
   Walter Kaufmann, PRINCETON UNIVERSITY   *23*

3. *The Contribution of Philosophy of the Social Sciences to Educational Development*
   Michael Scriven, INDIANA UNIVERSITY   *47*

4. *The Contribution of Philosophical Anthropology to Educational Development*
   Abraham Edel, THE CITY COLLEGE OF THE
          CITY UNIVERSITY OF NEW YORK   *69*

5. *Education and the Ideal of Personality*
   Peter A. Bertocci, BOSTON UNIVERSITY   *93*

6. *The Contribution of Philosophy to Educational Development: Summary, Commentary, and Projection*
   Kenneth D. Benne, BOSTON UNIVERSITY   *121*

INDEX   *151*

Foreword

In their attitudes toward educational theory, professional philosophers have traditionally distributed themselves into three groups. The first group has ignored it altogether, believing somehow that the ancient discipline of philosophy cannot properly concern itself with so mundane an affair as teaching and learning. In this category we could also place those individuals — from metaphysicians to language analysts — who continually redefine the enterprise of philosophy itself so as to exclude from its province the concerns of everyday men. The members of this first group represent the vast majority of those who have ever been or are at present engaged in philosophical inquiry.

A second group, considerably smaller, has ventured tentatively into the zones of educational thought most susceptible to general theorizing, such as the nature of human nature, the aims of education, or the general strategies by which men may realize their possibilities as men. Whitehead, Russell, and Maritain allowed themselves this much adventuring into the realm of educational ideas, and their example is being followed by a small but articulate scattering of contemporary thinkers.

The third group is smaller still, a limited contingent of philosophers who have come to see philosophical and educational problems as somehow continuous. As the chief exemplar of this group, John Dewey not only built much of the substructure of Experimentalism out of educational concepts but put forward the mind-boggling heresy that philosophy and education are really two aspects of the same undertaking — the forming of those fundamental dispositions toward nature and our fellow man which the world and experience demand of us. Eventually, Dewey and his coterie found themselves going far beyond educational aims and strategies to examine the relevance of philosophical thinking in curriculum design, teaching methodology, and administrative policy-making. Nor did they forget to suggest the reciprocal influence of pedagogical ideas on philosophical theorizing.

Our present-day space talk supplies an apt metaphor for this episode of intellectual history. Philosophy and education, hitherto traveling in separate orbits, have recently accomplished a successful rendezvous and docking maneuver, and — according to the view of this third group — their interests and concerns are now mutual and complementary.

The effects of the link-up have been various and not altogether expected. New turbulences have been generated in both parties, certainly. But also, it must be said, the making of common cause has tended to stabilize, in both fields, the production of ideas that men can use. In a world always too full of banality and high-minded irrelevance, this should count as some kind of progress.

But now we are beginning to witness a new staging of philo-sophic-educational ideas. A fourth generation, so to speak, of philosophers has taken up a new task: not the critical analysis of educational problems, from aims to methods, but rather the exploration of how education itself is studied, what kind of inquiry it is, and how its discipline is to be understood in the family of scholarship. In brief, the members of this fourth group are interested not so much in how schools should be conceived and conducted but in how educational inquiry itself should be conceived and conducted. They are seeking not a criticism of the educator's theories but rather a meta-criticism of his theorizing.

This book is one of the first of this new, fourth generation of philosophic-educational thinkers. The "educational development" of the title may suggest a certain ambiguity. The authors of these essays have used it to refer sometimes to the development of an individual's education and, at other times, to the development of educational institutions. In either case, however, the ultimate reference is to the development of education as a field of study and an object of scholarly interest to academic man. It is to this meaning of "development" that the book is addressed. As such, it is directed to all those for whom the study of education is a full-time professional task — psychologists, learning theorists, educational historians, sociologists, philosophers of education, methodologists, and pedagogical technicians.

Is the study of education an inquiry into behavior? Or is it concerned with the understanding of an extra-behavioral type of mental action?

Is education an applied social science? Or is it one of the humanities?

Is education concerned only with the cognitive? Or is it equally involved with the non-cognitive and emotive, and, if so, is there a canon of method equally appropriate for both spheres?

Is education a special case of enculturation? Or is it capable of supervening culture and speaking from a higher perch?

Is there an ideal of personality toward which educational thought is oriented? Or are there only local and proximate notions of the complete person?

Is the study of education in part the projection of man's future possibilities? Or is it only a ministry of assistance to society's other prophets?

These are some of the questions which this volume explores. Professors Aiken, Kaufmann, Scriven, Edel, Bertocci, and Benne have added measurably to our thinking on these and related concerns.

Van Cleve Morris

Editor's Introduction

The character of this century has been described as a revolution without revolutionaries. The characterization seems false on the face of it. Surely there have been revolutionaries, plenty of them, and of many kinds: anarchist, socialist, communist, fascist. Yet there are important senses in which the description is true. If it is taken to mean that events outran these doctrines, not that these beliefs had little or no part in shaping the world, then there is truth in it. Another interpretation might also fit the facts: it can be argued that the revolution was not as much the result of conscious social rebels as it was the unconscious doing of those who advanced science and technology, thereby creating a new world. Which were the more powerful revolutionaries, Marx and Engels, or science and technology? There is yet another sense in which the characterization holds true. In the United States, at least, the scientific and technological revolution was not led by revolutionary ideas but was met by the traditional wisdom. Society was transformed, but doctrine did not transform it.

In any case, all too often men have been wed to events without benefit of philosophy. Philosophy — frequently a latecomer, arriving after the deed has been done and history has been made — often only provides a doctrine to fit the state of affairs already established. As Hegel said, "When philosophy paints its grey in grey, one form of life has become old and by means of grey it cannot be rejuvenated, but only known. The owl of Minerva takes its flight only when the shades of night are gathering." Nevertheless, there is no natural law which dictates that philosophy must follow rather than lead events, and if men are to be the creators of their destiny rather than the creatures of their fate, ideas will have to lead rather than follow change. Revolutionaries will have to head revolutions. Otherwise, like leaders

xi

running to catch up with their followers, revolutionaries may have to race to overtake their revolutions. They then in fact will be post-revolutionaries or even counter-revolutionaries, for by that time events may have gone off on another course, leaving the original doctrines far behind them.

The future holds both the promise and threat of even more radical changes. Unless a miracle intervenes, the results of an aimless, non-rational, indeed unconscious revolution will be disastrous. Although events may always outrace thought, and though thought itself may err, a continuing revolution without revolutionaries endangers man needlessly, and, in the present situation, it may endanger him for the last time. Man will need all the resources that he can command if knowledge and wisdom are to guide the future. What are those resources? In particular, what can philosophy contribute?

The part philosophy might play is yet to be determined. As things stand now, all sorts of national and international policies and programs are being proposed in the name of "our" philosophy, but not with the advice, let alone the consent, of philosophers. It is not philosophers who whisper — or shout — into the ears of the mighty. At court they are nowhere to be seen, not even as jesters. Rather, they are notable for their absence. On the other hand, psychologists, political scientists, sociologists, anthropologists, and other social and behavioral scientists are engaged in making and carrying out social policy. These scientists not only go to Washington but they travel throughout the world advising on policy and administering programs of their own government and of foreign governments. Few statesmen these days — and they become ever fewer — would advocate an economic policy or program without consulting an economic adviser, even a whole Council of Economic Advisers. We have had a historian in the White House, have had and do have a science adviser to the President, but philosophers have we none. No national policy or program is now guided in any significant way, if at all, by a single philosopher, let alone by any Council of Philosophic Advisers. The counsel of philosophers is rarely sought at any level of statesmanship — local, state, or national — or in any field.

If philosophy were considered too important to be left to philosophers, the view might be mistaken as to who should rule the field, but at least the value of philosophy would not be in question. Or if it were contended that philosophy is indeed crucial but that philosophers should not be kings, the role of the philosopher might be at issue but not the status of philosophy itself. In both cases, the worth of philosophy would have been granted, and we could then turn to the questions of whose enterprise philosophy should be and what part philosophers should play in public affairs. As it is, however, philosophers are not only not kings but not even slaves; they are simply forgotten men, and they are so because philosophy itself is deemed of little or no consequence. Most philosophers are stuck away in universities, but even there they have little say, though they might have much *to* say. Even the increasing use of the interdisciplinary approach has made little difference, for philosophy is seldom included, either because it is considered an irrelevant discipline or no discipline at all.

If the rightful status of philosophy is to be determined, the state of philosophy itself must be examined. Traditionally, philosophy has sought to define the nature of the good life. Today, the quest for wisdom has in large part been superseded by the quest for clarity.[1] Thus, the task of the philosopher is not to develop a body of propositions but to clarify propositions. Philosophers no longer envision utopias. They do not develop comprehensive systems. Grand designs have been replaced by modest pieces of analysis. Philosophers now speak not with the authority of sages and seers but of logicians and linguistic assayers.

Analytic philosophy has become the most influential movement in American and English universities, not to mention its sway in other countries. Although many philosophers have rejoiced at this dominance, a number have despaired. Analytic

[1] Or if philosophy is still the love of wisdom, it is wisdom of another kind, to be found in a different place, through the use of different methods.

philosophers, contend the latter, are not concerned about the conduct of men, only about their language. They charge that for the analysts, the morals of men may be all wrong as long as their language is all right. The heavens may fall — no matter — but heaven help those whose language falls. This concern with the language of morals and not with morals itself, say these critics, is the disgrace of philosophy.

Bertrand Russell regards linguistic philosophy as a denial of philosophy. One of the severest critics of that philosophy, Ernest Gellner, has said, "A cleric who loses his faith abandons his calling, a philosopher who loses *his* redefines his subject." [2] The criticisms of Gellner and Russell, though shared by many philosophers who see their profession as falling into triviality, are no warrant for abandoning the analytic endeavor. The rise of one faith need not mean the loss of another. To adopt analysis is not to abandon the faith. There may now be a more substantial faith, because it is more inclusive. Conceivably, there might be a double faith or a joining of faiths, an ecumenism, so that the analytic and normative functions might both be served. Both undertakings are essential, and the problem may be seen as one of determining the distinctive contribution of each in relation to the other. Philosophy need not be, if indeed it ever was, exclusively analytic or normative.

But these considerations do not settle the issue. Even if they did, this issue, however significant, is only one aspect of a larger question: What can philosophy contribute to civilization as a whole and to its particular realms? To consider the question, "What can philosophy contribute to educational development?," the College of Education of Michigan State University held a conference in November, 1965. The chapters in this volume were originally prepared as papers for that conference.

The first contribution that philosophy might make is in answering the question, What is educational development? The first two papers, those of Professors Aiken and Kaufmann (Chapters 1 and 2), address that question from the points of view of analytic and normative philosophies respectively.

[2] Ernest Gellner, *Words and Things* (Boston: Beacon Press, 1960), p. 259.

Although philosophy of science as a whole has great relevance for educational development, philosophy of the social sciences is particularly significant. In his paper (Chapter 3) Professor Scriven discusses a number of issues in philosophy of the social sciences and points out the significance of the field for education, both methodologically and substantively.

It would be difficult to find any two areas more intimately related to educational development than those of culture and personality. Psychology has long been prominent in education. More recently, cultural anthropology has made its way into the field. The contribution of these sciences needs to be supplemented by that of the related philosophic fields, philosophical anthropology and philosophy of personality. In Chapter 4, Professor Edel examines the philosophic import for education of anthropological materials and methods of inquiry, and in Chapter 5, Professor Bertocci proposes an ideal of personality based upon value-experiences, each of which is distinctive but which in its proper union with other value-experiences, constitutes a harmonious, dynamic design.

Taken as a whole, what do these methods and fields of philosophy have to contribute to educational development? Professor Benne's summation (Chapter 6) sets out a cultural perspective from which to view the question, and from which to examine the relations that do hold and those that ought to hold between philosophers, on the one hand, and the prospective users of philosophy, the decision-makers, on the other. His paper provides a descriptive and critical summary, and also a projection of the possible future contribution of philosophy.

These papers not only yield some answers to the question of what philosophy can contribute to educational development; they also suggest a number of questions for subsequent investigation. Beyond that, they provide a renewed impetus to the continuing process of the evaluation of philosophy and its import for education.

George Barnett

PHILOSOPHY AND
EDUCATIONAL DEVELOPMENT

Chapter 1 / *Analytical Philosophy and Educational Development*

HENRY DAVID AIKEN

INTRODUCTION: PHILOSOPHICAL ANALYSIS AND ITS EDUCATIONAL USES

Before considering what the contribution of analytical philosophy to educational development may be, it is essential that something be said about analytical philosophy itself, its history, its varieties, its development. If my views sometimes seem peremptory and dogmatic, that is merely the result of an effort to be concise.

Let me say to begin with that I do not consider analytical philosophy to be more than an adjunct of philosophical activity. The often-concealed business of all philosophy, I am convinced, is with the wisdom and hence with the conduct of life, and especially with that form of education which is the condition of self-knowledge, self-development, self-transcendence, and self-control. Philosophy is not, properly, a subject or subject-matter, not a discipline, not a science, not even an art. This does not mean, of course, that philosophical reflection should not, or need not, be disciplined. Nevertheless, all philosophical inquiry that achieves its end of liberation must constantly move beyond the reach of all hitherto acquired disciplines, for philosophy, which is constantly preoccupied with limiting questions and with what lies beyond pre-established limits, finds existing disciplines insufficient to its purposes. By nature, any established discipline, including the disciplines of science and established religion, is inadequate to the aspirations of the philosopher toward self-knowledge and self-control. In attempting to deal with philosophical problems, we invariably find that our discipline and our disciplines are constantly breaking down and having to be repaired, supplanted, or even, on occasion, dispensed with altogether. Indeed, no discipline can be adequate to the endless crisis of human existence, which is the only perennial problem of philosophy.

Analytical philosophy is nothing new. In the *Euthyphro,* in which Socrates insistently raises questions about the meaning of piety; in the *Republic,* in which he makes all-important distinctions between questions about the meaning of justice and questions about the genesis, the uses, and, finally, the standards of justice; in the later dialogues, in which he attempts systematically to distinguish and to relate the concepts of being and non-being, of limit and the unlimited, of particular and universal, of appearance and reality, and of change and the permanent, Plato raises most of the questions which have occupied analytical philosophers since his time. What distinguishes Socrates and Plato is their sense of the relevance and even the necessity of such conceptual and logical analyses to the conduct of life. But as Plato shows, the philosopher is not, in one sense, a pure or disinterested analyst of ideas. In the *Parmenides,* for example, the concept of mud is considered, but only for purposes of illustration. What concerns the analytical philosopher is the forms of thought that guide our major forms of action. What constantly preoccupies him is the notions of the good, the true, the valid, the beautiful, the ideal, the noble, and the holy, in terms of which all of us articulate the ideals, standards, and procedures that govern our activities.

Plato, of course, did not and could not have the last word. If, as Whitehead contended, all subsequent philosophy is but a series of footnotes to Plato, the master notoriously raised more questions than he was able, or had the skills, to answer. And the footnotes, which get longer with every issue of *Mind,* are now more illuminating than the text. In short, analytical philosophy has had a long and extremely varied development, full of false starts and misconceptions, but also full of fruitful insights and fresh beginnings. Plato raised the major analytical questions, but he rarely succeeded in answering them; indeed, it is doubtful whether he or his followers grasped the nature or point of the questions they were raising. The philosophical analyst, to his sorrow, always finds that chief among the difficulties created by his predecessors are those arising from their preconceptions about the nature of analysis itself. In consequence, he is inevitably drawn into queries about the nature of nature, the analysis of analysis, the meaning of meaning. Here again, the opening moves were made by Plato. Philosophers have since gradually begun to work themselves free from Plato's own preconceptions about natures, analyses, and meanings, but they have done so laboriously and at great cost to the subsequent and interlocking histories of both philosophy and education.

Until the end of the nineteenth century, few philosophers understood that analytical philosophy must become, or acquire, a philosophy of expressions. Inevitably analytical philosophy, as it becomes more fully aware of what it is up to, turns, at least in part, into a linguistic philosophy, and this for the simple reason that, as Charles Sanders Peirce put it, "thought and expression are one." To understand a concept is to understand the meaning and the use of a form of expression; in practice, not even Plato could gaze on beauty bare. Peirce, however, also rightly insisted that not all forms of expression are linguistic, and hence that a general theory of expressions, which he, following Locke, called "semiotic," must make provision for many different types of signs, of which linguistic signs, such as they are, are only a special form. Where Peirce went radically wrong is in his assumption, inherited from Plato, that all meaningful expressions are signs, and hence that signification is the paradigmatic form of expression. In short, like most philosophers since Plato, Peirce was guilty of a pervasive and crippling error which might well be dubbed "the semanticist's error," that is, the error of supposing that the only, or proper, use of expressions, and particularly of verbal expressions, is to signify objects and to specify their characteristics and relations. This error is closely related to another, which in its turn may be called "the epistemologist's error." This is the mistake of supposing that the primary, or only proper business of discourse, and hence of thought, is to assert truths about the nature of things, and, correlatively, that the primary concern of the human mind itself is with the intuition, or else with the verification, of such truths. If anything has been learned from recent linguistic philosophy — although in fact it could have been learned long ago from George Berkeley and David Hume and Immanuel Kant — it is that human utterances have many characteristic or conventional roles, of which description, prediction, explanation, and analysis itself are merely the most conspicuous in a culture and in a tradition which, since Plato, has placed such an overwhelming emphasis upon cognition in general and theoretical science in particular.

Two tragic and consequent spiritual errors have attended the semanticist's and the epistemologist's errors. These may be called the errors of rationalism. One of them is the mistake of supposing that religion, art, morality, and philosophy are either putative forms of a super-science of being or reality or else, as it were, primitive proto-sciences which, in due course, will be replaced by genuine positive sciences, ready and able to give verifiable accounts of what there is. The other, counter-mistake of rationalists is to suppose that since, or in so far as, religion, art, morality, and philosophy are not sciences, or else are incapable of becoming sciences, they are at best peripheral or ancillary cultural activities and at worst sources of mythology, obscurantism, superstition, and irrationalism.

These rationalistic attitudes are widely and often unconsciously shared not only by the intellectuals and by men of letters who serve to propagate and to popularize the technical theories of the great philosophers, but also by educators at all levels of instruction, both formal and informal. To this day, as I have found to my cost, they dominate, or else confuse and distract, programs of general education that aspire to do "something more" than the various special sciences can decently provide, but are misled into supposing that the "something more"

in question must in principle be capable of justifying itself, if not
in scientific terms, then in the super-scientific terms of rationalistic philosophy, theology, and ethics. They are responsible for
conceptions of liberal, as distinct from technological and professional, education that reflect the classical view that the proper
concern of a free man, i.e., a citizen and a member of a leisured
class, is with the cultivation of his intellect and, through this,
with the contemplation of the truth. It is from this standpoint,
as it has developed in our own time, that the liberal arts are
still regarded as ancillary to the aims of research and the advancement of learning. And it is for this reason that the so-called
humanities have become increasingly, and particularly on the
side of academic preferment, departments of literary and cultural
history, of linguistics, semantics, and logic, and that departments
of fine arts and music have become departments of archeology,
art history, museum science, and musicology. Even within the
humanities, the cultivation of sensibility remains incidental and
accidental, and the concern with appreciation is left to young
instructors who have not yet fully outgrown their amateur
status as lovers of literature or art or music. Religion, where it
is not relegated to the divinity school (which itself still remains
in bondage to intellectualistic and scientistic theologies, the
effect of which is to breed either skepticism or soft-headedness),
becomes the province of a standing committee, usually com-
prised of historians, sociologists, and linguists, with perhaps a
logician or epistemologist thrown in to sweeten the pot. In most
liberal arts colleges outside the Bible Belt, the cultivation and
development of religious sensitivity and concern remains *infra
dig*, something which, because it is viewed either as not seriously
concerned with what exists or else as concerned only with sup-
positious or supernatural entities beyond the range of scientific or
historical scrutiny, has no proper place in the formal academic
curriculum.

There remains, however, an uneasy feeling on the part of most
educators that while the "facts" are pretty well taken care of by
the various special sciences, something called "values" is not.
But how to take care of them without embarrassment in an aca-

demic context except "objectively," i.e., through the respectable methods of historical, anthropological, sociological, and now logical and semantical analysis, remains a question to which our committees on educational policy have found no satisfactory answers. Curiously, the one type of school which, to its own satisfaction at least, provides an alternative to the diffident eclecticism of our public and secular schools, namely, the Catholic parochial school, is itself the victim of a classical semanticism, epistemologism, and rationalism which in their own ways reduce, or aspire to reduce, values to facts and moral principles to a kind of natural law. Such an alternative, I am convinced, cannot survive the scrutiny of contemporary philosophical analysis. And where an attempt has been made to introduce it into the non-Catholic university, as happened for example at the University of Chicago during the era of Hutchins and Adler, the result has served merely to discredit the whole effort to provide responsible ethical and evaluative instruction in the schools of higher learning.

Meanwhile, in the secondary schools, desultory, insensitive, and dogmatic programs of instruction, or indoctrination, in the civic values and virtues of the existing political and social establishment leave the student quite unprepared for the arduous tasks of moral and ideological reconstruction, upon which depend the possibility of orderly, progressive social change. In an age of unparalleled technological development, of social and political revolution that involves whole continents, and of murderous ideological conflicts, the average high-school graduate, for all his learning, is wholly untrained for the continuing work of individual and collective deliberation, without which democracy itself remains merely another form of oppression, and civil liberties merely protective covering for the advertiser and the propagandist.

These remarks must not be misunderstood. I have no illusions about the ability of analytical and linguistic philosophy alone to offset the monumental intellectual confusions and spiritual disorders that seem to me to be inherent in our major Western cultural traditions. The analytical philosopher, like his great exemplar, remains essentially a midwife; he offers merely the possibility of a clearer head, a freer imagination, a more receptive sensibility. He does not offer salvation; he cannot provide a faith; he cannot remove the economic and social causes of human alienation and oppression. Let me also emphasize, that, although I think it is indeed one of the functions of a wise linguistic philosopher to offset the errors of the semanticist, the epistemologist, and the scientific methodolatrist, it by no means follows that he is, or should be, hostile either to science itself or to knowledge, or to those forms of discourse which are indispensable to science and to the inculcation and spread of knowledge. The proper aim of linguistic philosophy should be to refine and to clarify our conceptions of the life of reason, not to oppose it. It is the business of the linguistic philosopher to determine the terms and the limits of rational judgment and action, not to propose alternatives to them. Irrationalism is as profound an error as rationalism, and the mind that despises science is unfit for philosophy itself.

EDUCATIONAL DEVELOPMENT: ITS MEANING, CONDITIONS, AND LIMITS

Now I must come more directly to terms with our subject. What I propose to do in the pages immediately following is (1) to offer an account of the concept of educational development — its use, its range, its varieties, and its limits; (2) to say something about the idea of the teacher — what he must do, what he can and cannot do within the process of educational development; and (3) to indicate some of the logical conditions of learning — what it is to learn and not to learn, and what perhaps cannot be learned and hence what falls outside the range of educational development. In the course of my remarks I hope to show how limited is an education which confines itself to the purveying of information — what William James called "knowledge about" and Gilbert Ryle calls "knowing that"; I hope also to show how much, even within the sphere of theoretical education, generally depends upon the acquisition of skills and the development of aptitudes — in short, upon much that goes, somewhat pejoratively but without justification, under such headings as mere "training," "vocational education," "professional education," or "technological education." The greater part of all education, as I shall argue, is and must be a matter of training and of forms of teaching and learning that now pass as merely vocational, professional, and technological. At the same time, I intend to question the value to the learner of an information-oriented education, even within the domain of science itself.

When we glance at the etymology of the term "education" we are immediately confronted with the question of whether the phrase "educational development" is not pleonastic. It is worth recalling that the Latin root of the word "education" and its cognates is the verb "*educere*," which means simply to lead or to bring forth, and hence, in at least one obvious sense, to develop. And it is significant that our word "educe" is also derived from "*educere*," for initially "education" seems simply to be a virtual synonym for "development." From this point of view, one is tempted simply to say that a person's educational development and his education are one and the same thing, and hence that an analysis of the idea of educational development would have to be coordinate with the analysis of the concept of education itself. Nor, up to a point, is the temptation to be resisted, for, as we shall see, the word "education" covers a lot of ground, from which, initially, nothing pertaining to the rearing of the young, or at any rate the undeveloped, can reasonably be excluded.

Upon reflection, however, one perceives at least a distinction between educational development and other forms of development that is germane to our purpose. For one is bound, I think, to resist the suggestion that the concept of education applies naturally to the maturation of the organism, and in particular the physical body, through ordinary ineluctable processes of growth and assimilation. It may well be, therefore, that a main point of discussions of educational development should be to underline the central differences between education as a developmental process and other modifications or changes to which organisms, and particularly human organisms, are subject. For example it would be entirely pertinent in a study in depth of the process of educational development to examine the ways in which other developmental processes set limits to, or else positively impede, what can be accomplished through education. Or, again, it might be worthwhile, in certain contexts, to elaborate the ways in which the levels of natural development or maturation must be carefully taken into account in intelligently planning the formal educational development of men from kindergarten, through the secondary schools, to the college, the university, and the graduate school. In spite of all this, however, the primary fact remains that there can be no form of education which is non-developmental, and that any teacher who leaves the minds and hearts of his pupils just where they were has taught them nothing at all.

To overstate a point in order to make one, I suggest that the sphere of education and hence of educational development is coterminous with that of mental action. Even so-called physical education, which by definition involves the training and the manipulation of the body, would not, I think, be called a form of education were modes of mental action, and hence of mental aptitude and skill, not also essentially involved. A child's foot that has a tendency to be pigeon-toed can, in a sense, be "trained" to walk normally. But in so far as this involves merely the exertion of mechanical pressures with corresponding bodily changes, one would, I think, be properly disposed to resist calling such a process or development "educational." Hence, I shall contend, as a general thesis, that all education whatever involves, if indeed it does not implicitly aim at, some form of mental action and the acquisition of the skills and aptitudes, as well as the achievements, essential to such forms of action.

If this is so, the term "education" and its cognates themselves belong to the sphere of what the English call "psychological," as distinct from purely physical, or physicalistic, expressions. I myself prefer simply to say that "education" and its cognates can be fully explicated only within, and in the light of, a general analytical philosophy of mind. From this the important consequence follows that any analysis of educational concepts which attempts to define them in purely bodily or physical terms, or, alternatively, which supposes that the theory of education could be part of, or else reduced to, something which is nowadays called "behavioral science," is systematically misguided. The reason for this, however, has nothing to do with the metaphysical doctrine, of which I, at least, wish no part, that implies that the mind is a ghostly substance to which the individual consciousness alone has immediate access and which other persons can penetrate only symptomatically, if at all. The claim I am making is not, in the first instance, at least, ontological, but logical and semantical. For I am contending only that the development of minds, and hence educational development, cannot be properly discussed or understood exclusively in physicalistic terms. And I am arguing that although certain physical changes are normally or typically correlated with mental changes, and although, therefore, there are certain physical conditions of mental and, hence, educational achievement, it is a radical error to suppose that mental changes are nothing but physical changes or that meeting certain physical conditions simply as such is all that we mean by mental or educational achievement. Education per se is a mental process, and the logic of meaningful discourse about education and educational development, accordingly, is not and cannot be discourse about mere bodily changes or developments. And it is precisely for this reason that the whole philosophy of educational testing, including not only the testing of actual performance, but also testing for aptitudes, is in need of a complete conceptual overhaul.

There are also other directions in which it is of the utmost importance to oppose reductivistic analyses of the concept of educational development. Here I have in mind particularly the tendency in some quarters to reduce the educational process to that of formal and informal instruction. Educational development, or, more simply, education itself involves not only formal and informal instruction of the learner by a teacher, but also what the anthropologist calls "enculturation." By "enculturation," I take it, the anthropologist has in mind the processes, in large part passive and unintentional, through which most individuals acquire the attitudes and propensities, linguistic or otherwise, that characterize them as mature members of various social groups. As we say, "experience is a great teacher." What this means, among other things, is that by the ordinary wear and tear of living in societies, through an immense variety of what we somewhat animistically call "agencies," human beings learn, and learn to adapt themselves to, the myriad rules, laws, and principles, the learning of which constitutes the greater part of "growing up."

For our purposes, the notion of enculturation is useful precisely because it enables us to correct not only the common tendency to overintellectualize the process of educational development, but also to overstress the role of purposive and intentional action even within the sphere of informal education which occurs outside the school. As such, educational development properly involves not only the results of specialized courses of instruction in particular subjects or subject-matters, or even of thoughtful parental training that results in the acquisition of skills, linguistic and otherwise, without which formal education itself could not even exist; it encompasses also the results of enculturative processes of identification, of uncontrolled suggestion and association, which not even the most perfect totalitarian system could conceivably control. Indeed, it is largely through a study of the concept of educational development, as I have lately come to see, that we are enabled to overcome the nightmare of a society of human robots, "educated" by their masters to do, think, and act in certain routine ways from which every "outside" influence is excluded. Once we realize, in fact, how little of what we all learn depends upon instruction, we are freed from the gratuitous worry that a system of instruction, beginning with infant toilet training, could, even in principle, turn out a class of creatures capable of nothing but following the rules which their teacher-masters have set for them. The learning process necessarily outruns any process of instruction, whether formal or informal. And for better as well as for worse, the educational development of no man can ever be exclusively a matter of deliberate, institutionalized routines. Accordingly, the term "educators" must include not only human instructors and teachers but also institutions, practices, and indeed all of the agencies, personal, interpersonal, and impersonal, that serve as media for the formation, development, and reformation of the mind. In other terms, education is a process before it is an agency, and it remains a vehicle of self-development long after the last course has been taken and the last examination has been passed.

But now I want to propose a second general thesis which, I believe, is implicit in what has already been said. The thesis is this: the sphere of a person's educational development is virtually coterminous with the development of his sensitivity to meanings. Whatever serves to structure a person's awareness of meanings or to enlarge the range of meanings to which he is responsive belongs distinctively to his education, and hence to his educational development. In short, wherever there is a mode of meaning, there is a corresponding possibility of educational development. Accordingly, failures or blockages in the educational process are all, in one way or another, failures or blockages of the process of assimilating the meanings or modes of meaning that the environment offers our minds for understanding and use. If this is so, however, the limits of the educational process are reached whenever one passes beyond the domain of meaning into spheres of purely instinctual reaction, of unalterable bodily change, and of organic insensitivity or unresponsiveness.

Teaching, Telling, and "Enculturation"

From what has been said, a basis has already been provided for seeing why those who are concerned with the whole idea of education and with the educational process as a whole must at once realize how much of the education of any person or group proceeds, and must proceed, without benefit of teachers, of schooling, or indeed of instruction of any sort whatever. This may have its saddening, or even frightening, aspect when one thinks of the educations which life in a city slum or in a country rent by the savagery of war automatically and inescapably affords. But it also has its happy or at least its hopeful side when one bears in mind the ways in which a progressive culture, enlightened institutions, and an open, amiable, and peaceful social milieu may itself serve in myriad ways to educate the human spirit and to compensate for the limitations under which, for one reason or another, the formal educational system may labor.

Either way, we see why the teacher is something at once more and less than the "educator," and why teaching, no matter how skillful or extensive, can only be a part of education. For education may go on without a teacher or even, as we have seen, without any person to do the educating. Or to put the point in another way, if we agree, at least for the sake of discussion, to treat the concepts of teacher and student as coordinate ideas, so that every teacher must have a student and every student a teacher, then we may see why only a part of our education is owing to what we are taught as students, and why teaching must always remain only a special part of education, even in the most abundant society endowed with the amplest supply of skilled and dedicated teachers.

Except in an incidental, metaphorical sense in which, inevitably, we personify any educative factor as a "teacher," teaching is something done by individual "persons." Plainly, there is no teaching without a teacher, and no teachers except individual organisms. A dog, as well as a man perhaps, may teach, but, strictly speaking, institutions, cultures, societies, or natural environments cannot. We must distinguish, however, not only between those teachers who do their teaching within the framework of the formal educational institution which we call the school, and those who teach more informally outside such a framework, but also between forms of teaching in which what is learned is a consequence of what the teacher aims to teach, and those forms in which what is learned (and taught) is not such a consequence. I may teach you something more, or less, than I mean to teach. Correspondingly, you may learn from me, as a teacher, what I never meant to teach, and I may teach

you more, as well as less, than my tour of duty as a teacher per-
mits or requires.

But now we have been provided with one way of distinguishing between teaching a subject and teaching a person. Any
teacher must teach somebody; unless some person or persons are
instructed, teaching cannot occur. But there may be teaching,
and indeed powerful and important teaching, without a subject.
Socrates was a great teacher, but he had no subject to teach.
Few of us, unfortunately, are disciples of Socrates. But all of
us teachers who do have subjects to teach, organized information to impart, and methods to inculcate, may nevertheless teach
much more than our subjects or disciplines or methods include,
and indeed more than we mean to teach or even imagine ourselves capable of teaching.

Here we begin to trench upon what may well turn out to be
one of the central issues of an analytic philosophy of education.
Professor Israel Scheffler, who has perhaps done more than anyone else to advance interest in the analytical philosophy of
education, makes a sharp distinction not only between teaching
and enculturation but also between teaching and telling. Without going into details, I think that the central point of Scheffler's position is that teaching as distinct from enculturation or
mere telling (and hence education in the broad sense) involves
something more than what psychologists call "conditioning," as
well as something more than making students aware of ideas or
meanings. That is to say, a teacher not only shows something to
his students, he also explains, or is capable of explaining what he
has shown; a teacher not only tells but gives, or is capable of
giving, reasons for believing that what he tells is true or valid or
correct. In a word, the teacher, as distinct from what may be
called the mere "teller" or even in the broadest sense, the mere
educator, always provides, or is capable of providing, a rationale
for his instruction. And when the teller or the educator, as I
shall call him, is incapable of giving reasons, of providing a rationale, of invoking a method or a way of doing things in order
to justify what he says or shows, he fails by that much to attain
the stature of teacher.

For the sake of discussion let us, a bit tendentiously, call this the "rationalistic" theory of teaching. And now, by way of contrast to it, let me briefly describe what may be called simply the anti-rationalistic theory of teaching.[1] By this I have in mind the point of view which not only does not regard the giving of reasons, or even the capacity to give them, as essential to or inherent in the activity of teaching, but which, for whatever reason, actually depreciates the whole gestalt of reason-giving, or justification and explanation, of method-mongering, as positively inimical to the aims of the teacher, at least along the higher reaches on which he may aspire to move. Thus, for example, the teacher who seeks to inspire his students, whether by his eloquence, by his example, or by his general comportment, is perhaps bound to be an anti-rationalist and thus to depreciate the whole tedious, discursive side of formal education. And in justification of his own work, he, like William James, is likely to stress (or overstress) the happy improvisations, both of word and gesture, which the particular topic or circumstance happens to suggest.

I think that although the issue between the rationalist and the anti-rationalist may be clarified, it cannot be settled entirely by the methods of logical or semantical analysis because the issue between them is not, at bottom, entirely a logical or semantical issue. As far as I can see, the concept of teaching does not positively require that the teacher be capable of providing a rationale or explanation of what he seeks to impart; further, it may well be that certain forms of teaching can proceed only by way of example, by a process of "showing," for which there are no linguistic equivalents and for which no reasons are available. To this extent I think that logic is on the side of the anti-rationalists. But when he goes beyond this to contend that "true" or "real" or "significant" teaching, or teaching of the most significant or important subjects, cannot proceed discursively, or else that discursive explanations provide a positive hindrance, he is claiming

---

[1] *Prima facie*, these theories, I should emphasize, are presented as opposing theories of the meaning of the idea or concept of teaching. Whether they really are so remains to be seen.

more than the logic of our discourse about teaching requires. Indeed, what he is doing is attempting to deflate (or else to inflate) a certain mode of teaching, or the sort of subject-matter to which that mode naturally lends itself, under the guise of philosophical analysis.

How does this happen? Is there not some important feature of the notion of a teacher which has so far escaped our notice and which, for whatever reason, positively invites those of us who have educational or pedagogical, and hence developmental, axes to grind, to grind them into the very texture of our thinking about educational problems? The answer, I believe, is that the term "teacher" and its cognates, particularly in cultures which, like our own, set great store by the institution of the school and by the teaching process, both as a means and as a model for achieving desirable social ends, are not purely descriptive terms that serve to neutrally characterize ordinary things or processes. Built into the notion of the teacher is the idea of someone who does something desirable or exemplary, of someone who serves an important cause or end, or who performs a function of merit or value within the community. To say that one is a "teacher," in short, is not merely to describe one's occupation, what one does, for better or for worse, but also to lay a flattering umbrage to one's soul, to claim for oneself a certain status together with the privileges or rights pertaining thereto. Likewise, to say that someone is not a teacher is, in at least certain contexts, automatically to disparage him or his work. And if it can be "shown" that he is not a "true" or a "real" teacher, then automatically he is declassed.

In saying this, however, I do not claim that the word "teacher" and its cognates serve merely as terms of praise or that their meaning is merely "emotive." Indeed, the whole concept of emotive meaning seems to me to be at once too coarse and too misleading to serve any longer as a useful rubric of philosophical analysis. What I contend is only that in ascribing or assigning the teacher's role to a person one is, at the same time, laying upon him certain responsibilities and entitling him to certain rights or prerogatives.

THE LEARNER: "LEARNING THAT" VERSUS "LEARNING HOW"; MODES OF MEANING AND MODES OF LEARNING

So far we have dealt only in passing and by implication with the primary object, or product, of the whole process of educational development, namely, the educatable and educated person. In concluding these remarks, it is essential to say something about him, partly in order to distinguish aspects of the process that have hitherto been neglected and partly in order to make clear what lies beyond the process of educational development. Here, among other things, I want to deflate the importance for educational development of merely "learning about" or "learning that." Even for those who seek instruction in the most advanced and abstract reaches of theoretical science, learning how and learning why are continually indispensable.

This is not to say that education should be exclusively concerned with questions of method. For the study of methods is meaningless and pointless save in so far as the methods are actually used in making significant inquiries that lead to the formation of hypotheses, theories, and doctrines. Moreover, there is a great danger in certain quarters that students may be led into that fatal sin of methodolatry, the worship of the procedure or routine, which itself can stultify the advancement of learning. Methods are to be viewed as being in continuous interaction with the results they yield and with the ends they serve, and therefore as themselves subject to modification when they run into conflict with other no less exigent commitments. Again, to overstate a point in order to make one, nothing that is learned, or learnable, should be viewed as incorrigible, as beyond the pale of critique and of criticism. I like to think that an analogue of the naturalistic fallacy hovers, or should be made to hover, over the whole *idea* of education as well as over the entire system of concepts affiliated with it. Anywhere, at any time, we may in all seriousness echo the ancient cry, "But is it, after all is said and done, really right, really valid, really proper, really true?" Of course, the open question becomes a silly question, which is to say, not a question at all, when asked idly or compulsively or tendentiously. Nor am I suggesting that serious people should raise it whenever they feel a minor irritation with "the system" as it stands. My contention is again that every a priori is so only for the time being and every pre-emptive certitude can be made to yield under stress. And, in a word, the stress here upon learning how is intended not so much to enthrone method as the only proper subject-matter of instruction, but rather to underline the point that within the sphere of theoretical learning itself, learning about the nature of things is largely valueless, if not strictly impossible, unless one at the same time learns how such theoretical understanding is acquired.

But now we must come once again to cases. To begin with, just as we were obliged to distinguish teachers from mere educators, so also we must distinguish students from mere learners. If the end of education in a sense is learning, that end will not be served simply by trying to make students of us all. The student requires a teacher; the learner as such does not. Indeed, it may well be that the most urgent educational need is for teachers to enable their students to continue as learners, on their own, after their courses of instruction and of study have long since been forgotten. The point is obvious, but it is important both conceptually and practically. For the educational process has made a fetish of the student and with the studies, and courses of study, to which he is submitted. Not the instruction of students, but the learning of men is the over-arching business of education. The learner, by definition, can only be a student part-time. But it is what he learns the rest of the time which usually matters most, both to himself and to his fellows.

The learner, we may say, is a would-be knower. His primary business as a learner is with knowledge. Unfortunately, however, this is perhaps the most misleading statement a philosopher of education can make. For the concept of knowledge has been so badly misanalyzed and misconceived in our western philosophical tradition that it might almost be better to say that the business of the learner is more with feeling or volition or sen-

sibility than with something called "cognition." In the first
place, knowing is not confined to, if indeed it has anything to do
with, what rationalistic philosophers call "intuition." In the second place, knowing as such is not a matter of certainty or of
being certain. In the third place, it is not, as such, remotely a
matter of theoretical understanding. And finally, there is no such
thing as the seat or faculty or organ of knowledge, nor is that
seat or faculty or organ properly described as the intellect, the
faculty of reason, or the faculty of judgment. Knowledge, above
all and first of all, is an achievement. Secondly, as an achievement, it exists in degree, and hence in varying degrees. Thirdly,
it is a form of achievement which is open not only to theoretical
mathematicians, physicists, and sociologists, but also to people
who can barely count, to people who play the flute, who make
decisions, contracts, promises, judgments, who perform opera-
tions — in short, who do anything that involves what we call
"know-how" — the acquisition of skills, the understanding and
ability to conform to rules or routines, to enact, to engage in
practices, to assume roles, responsibilities, and obligations, to
adopt policies, and, in a word, to do all the myriad things which
are connoted by the phrase "knowing how," and hence "learning how." On this score, indeed, a large and fundamental point
can be summarily made by saying that one great province of
educational development, and that by all odds the most important and the most extensive, concerns the endless and endlessly
various business of knowing and of learning how.

This is not in the least meant to minimize the significance of
"knowing that" and hence of "learning that" in our educational
scheme of things. My interest here is of another order. For, in
the first place, when one fully appreciates how much of any person's education, even on its theoretical side, is concerned with, or
depends upon, learning how to do things, one is then less disposed to overstress the importance of sheer "learning," as scholars
rather curiously call it, within the process of educational development. But in the second place, when we attend more closely
to what is comprehended under the concepts of learning how

(and learning why),[2] we see more clearly how specious is the claim, reiterated by rationalists in all ages, that the only or primary business of education, and hence of the educated man, must be with the pursuit of truth, and particularly of theoretical truth. Indeed, we may see how specious and dangerous is the very notion that it is the business of education, including in particular the so-called higher learning, to advance learning, either individually or collectively. Learning how is indispensable, although not sufficient, to doing anything well.

But it is precisely for this reason that an educational system which is directed only to forms of learning how that are necessary to doing theoretical science is in fact neglecting three-fourths of its responsibility. The fact that our culture produces so many learned monsters and so many educated fools is owing very largely, in my judgment, to the deep-rooted blunder of placing what my old colleague Morton White calls "the teacher of knowing," as distinct from "the teacher of feeling or willing," in the driver's seat in our educational system and of rewarding so heavily "the student of knowing" as distinct from the "student of feeling or willing." Or, rather, since this way of talking is itself so deeply misleading, let me return to my own point that even if, perhaps, all instruction aims at knowledge and all learning results in knowing, all instruction does *not* aim, directly or indirectly, at cultivating and informing something called "the intellect."

The point toward which these remarks have been drifting is simply this: if all meaning either is or involves expression, and if the meaning of all expressions and all modes of expression must somehow be *learned*, then, plainly what learning, and hence educational development, covers is everything that essentially involves the use and application of expressions or what I sometimes call "meaning carriers." This means that the limits of educational development are set only by the limits of our powers of learning in regard to the use of expressions or meaning carriers.

[2] In this paper I do no justice to knowing and learning why. But no account of education and educational development can afford to neglect them.

What are these limits? In general, they are reached whenever we come to the performance of a particular act, to the making of a particular decision, to the adoption of a particular policy, to the composition of a particular poem or sonata, and to the whole sphere to which such words as "discovery," "creation," and "invention" apply. After the fact, discoveries, works of creation, products of invention are proper materials for the learner's educational development. But one cannot learn to discover, to create, or to invent, any more than one can learn to live or to die.

The moral point here is not only that, like Virgil, all teachers, and indeed all educators, must finally bid farewell to their pupils, who must thereafter go it on their own, but also that the learner himself must not expect everything from his education or be perversely disappointed when it appears to "fail" him. Maturity comes when one has learned *both* the necessary competencies *and* the necessity of moving on one's own, beyond the range of competence. Learning can continue throughout life, but it is not life. Educational development can progress until senility sets in, but even in one's youth neither education nor learning can be all. What one must learn at last and above all is that one must cease, and continually cease, to be a learner. In America, where so much has been invested in education, both materially and spiritually, this last lesson should never be forgotten. The good society, like the good man, is something which not even the most affluent and resourceful educational system can produce on order. And this too is something which all rationalists since Plato have had a hard time learning. The school does not, any more than the military camp or the church or the music hall, provide a proper model for the good or the just society. For the good society, like the good life, has no models. And though a society might just conceivably learn how to be "great," according to the preconceptions of one pundit or another, its worth is another matter which only the gods are able to decide.

Chapter 2 / *Educational Development from the Point of View of a Normative Philosophy*

WALTER KAUFMANN

If I understand the topic assigned to me correctly, I have been invited to lay down the law — of course, without any presumption that anyone will accept it. Professor Aiken has been asked to analyze the question, while I have been asked to answer it by saying what educational development ought to be. Under ordinary circumstances I should certainly be inclined to analyze the question — if only as a defensive reflex, to gain time and put off a difficult commitment.

Indeed, the question "What is educational development?" seems so ambiguous, it might be said to cry out for analysis. "Educational development" could refer to the development of education, especially of methods of education, or to the development of human beings in the course of their education. These two seemingly quite different developments, however, can be viewed as two aspects of the same thing: kinds of education differ insofar as they lead students to develop differently. Theoretically, two different systems of education, one earlier and the other a later development, might differ greatly in expensiveness but scarcely at all in their effects on the students' development; but I plan to discuss methods of education that have different consequences for the students' development, especially at the college level.

This calls for one crucial reservation at the outset. Much education, particularly at the college level, is self-education that owes more to the library and to extra-curricular experiences and discussions than to the faculty or curriculum. This assertion need not be based exclusively on personal recollection and observation: there is a vast literature on the development of artists, writers, and other individuals who owe little to formal education and much to personal experience and experiments and to self-chosen models. It includes autobiographies, biographies, and many remarkable novels. There is even a special name for novels of this type: *Bildungsroman,* which might be rendered as "novel of educational development." This genre has been cultivated by many of the best German novelists, often in tomes of considerable bulk. One such novel, however, is as brief as it is brilliant: Hermann Hesse's *Siddhartha.* Here Hesse calls into question the possibility of helping a creative person by means of direct teaching, at least as far as our fundamental orientation and way of life are concerned; but he also shows, if a little less obviously, how an encounter with a great teacher whose explicit doctrine is not accepted may nevertheless haunt a man through his whole life, affecting it for the better.

It is the beginning of wisdom to recognize the limits of education, quite especially at the college level. Administrators often overestimate the influence of educational systems and changes in required courses of study on men and women around the age of twenty. It is well to recall the words often attributed to the Jesuits: "Give us a child until the age of five, and you can have it for the rest of its life." Psychoanalysts from Freud to Bruno Bettelheim have lent strength to this suggestion. There is also some point to the story of the middle-aged alumnus who expressed his heartfelt thanks to an old professor: "Nobody else has influenced me as much as you; I have never forgotten what you used to say; you have changed my life." "And what," asked the professor, "did I say?" The alumnus told him, and the old teacher replied: "But I said precisely the opposite."

Nevertheless, teachers also discover, at least occasionally, that their words, both spoken and written, have had some influence — no doubt less than many had hoped for when young, but more than they had supposed in moments, or periods, of depression.

The rhetorical question, "Have you ever heard of anybody changing his mind on the basis of an argument?" is preposterously
misleading: students, and even their elders, frequently change
their views in the light of arguments and evidence. And as long
as educators have *some* influence, it is worthwhile to ask what
can be done to make it beneficial rather than harmful.

It seems to be my assignment to venture some normative suggestions, and I have accepted this assignment, although I do not
believe that it is felicitous to distinguish analytical philosophy
and normative philosophies. Oddly, this antithesis goes back to
Nietzsche, who once protested that "people should finally stop
confounding philosophical laborers, and scientific men generally,
with philosophers." He distinguished "the scientific laborers of
philosophy" who follow "the noble model of Kant and Hegel"
from "genuine philosophers" who are "legislators: they say, 'thus
it shall be!'" Even Nietzsche conceded, however, that "it may
be necessary for the education of a genuine philosopher that he,
too, has once stood himself on all these steps on which . . . the
scientific laborers of philosophy remain standing"; and at the end
of this aphorism he insinuated that there neither were nor ever
had been as yet "genuine philosophers" in the sense here described, though he expected such philosophers to appear in the
future. This whole aphorism[1] seems to me much inferior to the
one immediately following, in which the great task of philosophers past and present is described as "being the bad conscience of their time. By applying the knife vivisectionally to
the chest of the very virtues of their time, they betrayed what
was their own secret: to know of a new greatness of man, of a
new untrodden way to his enhancement." Nietzsche then described Socrates as an example of such a philosopher and concluded the aphorism by considering the task of a present-day
philosopher.

As the second of these two aphorisms implies, unlike the first,
we find both analyses and normative suggestions in the work of
the major moral philosophers from Socrates, Plato, and Aristotle
to Spinoza and Kant, Mill and Russell. "Normative" thinkers or

[1] Friedrich W. Nietzsche, *Beyond Good and Evil* (1886), Section 211.

"legislators" who are not also analysts are not philosophers. Instead of contrasting analytical and normative philosophers, we should contrast those who are *merely* analysts and those who are both analytic and normative philosophers; and I do not believe that any of the major moral philosophers belong in the first category.

Even such an antithesis may be inferior to the image of a continuum in which we can distinguish differences in degree. Most philosophers have an implicit vision of what man might become; but not all of them make this normative vision explicit, and even some who do spell it out do so only in *obiter dicta* or, it seems, unintentionally. Since World War II it has become the fashion not to speak explicitly in the normative mode, and I have probably been asked to discuss educational development "from the point of view of a normative philosophy" because in a chapter on morality in one of my books I ventured to propose not only some analyses but also four cardinal virtues: humbition (a fusion of humility and ambition, neither of which I consider a virtue without the other), courage, love, and honesty.[2]

Perhaps I was expected to suggest that educational development should consist in the development of these virtues. Naturally, I should welcome any education that succeeded in attaining these goals (I dare say, you would, too); and I believe that humility and honesty, and even love, can be taught to some extent, even after the age of five. Ambition and courage, which depend heavily on vitality and self-confidence, may present far greater problems, at least at the college level. Nor do I believe that I am merely grinding a personal axe when I commend an education that develops humility, love, and honesty: in a crucial sense, education has failed when men and women do not emerge with a sense of their own limitations and fallibility; with widened sympathies and a resolve to try to understand, as from the inside, much that at first seems strange and odious; and with a sharpened intellectual conscience. But I shall not go on to offer a syllabus at this point — not because I wish to

---

[2] *The Faith of a Heretic* (New York: Doubleday & Company, Inc., 1961), Sections 83–86.

eschew controversy on specifics but because a liberal arts education is on the whole designed to develop these qualities. Even
love is taught in a sense — not in chapel but by reading Aeschylus, Shakespeare, and Tolstoy, for example. The Athenian poet
makes us see the Persians whom he fought, who killed his
brother and sacked Athens, as essentially human beings whose
sufferings are as genuine and heart-rending as our own; and in
this respect his tragedy, *The Persians*, is a paradigm of much
of the greatest literature.

I have touched the major themes I wish to develop, but I do
not want to go on to justify present-day curricula — the inclu-
sion of literature and comparative religion or the assignment of
Dostoevsky or the Dhammapada, for instance. Instead of defending what stands in no need of defense, what is good and
widely acknowledged to be so, I want to address myself to a
more basic problem and propose some changes.

THE ANALYTICAL AND THE HISTORICAL APPROACH

It is now fashionable among philosophers in the English-
speaking world to suppose that analysis is difficult, but that
saying how things ought to be (which is too readily equated with
preaching) is easy. In fact, the analytical approach is comparable to the historical approach which has dominated much of German thought since Hegel: it allows one to avoid controversy
about matters of consequence; one postpones, often indefinitely,
sticking out one's neck; and all the while one can claim to be
scientific — *wissenschaftlich*.

Armed with the historical approach, one can discuss any idea
or concept, provided one either knows the history of philosophy
well or has the time to check what a few notables have said
about this notion or how they have used it. Armed with the
analytic approach, one does not even have to know the history
of philosophy, nor does one require a library. What one needs
is a technique — not a full-blown method but rather something
like a knack — and one has to know the language well enough
to know how words are used properly.

It would be silly to denigrate either of these two approaches: both historical perspective and analysis — preferably not exclusively linguistic — are invaluable, and as long as we ignore either we are likely to come to grief. Therefore it is entirely legitimate and even crucially important to teach students both history and analysis, and to have recourse to both when confronted with a difficult question.

This may sound as conciliatory as the old Emperor Franz Joseph of Austria is said to have been in his senility: he told the plaintiff he was right, he told the defendant he was right, and when it was pointed out to him that both could not very well be right, he said, "That is right, too." But my point is not that both approaches are right in isolation but rather that each is imperfect without the other. Recalling Kant's famous dictum, "Thoughts without contents are empty, intuitions without concepts are blind," [3] we might say: history without analysis is inconclusive, and analysis without history is blind. Ideas should be studied and understood in their historical setting and context, but they should also be taken seriously enough to be analyzed, and if they are confused or ambiguous, that could be shown. But even when these two approaches are fused, do they suffice? Or is something further needed?

Schopenhauer and Nietzsche have remarked that "preaching morals is just as easy as giving reasons for morals is difficult"; [4] and the same point has been made by others, too. Because it is difficult to back up normative judgments — much more difficult than handling either the historical or the analytical approach competently — those who offer normative judgments often merely preach, giving either no reasons or bad reasons, and historians and analysts sometimes talk as if value judgments were tied to the homiletic mode.

If all normative judgments were bound to be merely emotive, they would seem to belong in the chapel rather than the class-

[3] Immanuel Kant, *Critique of Pure Reason* (1781), p. 51; (1787), p. 75.
[4] Arthur Schopenhauer, *Über den Willen in der Natur* (1836), p. 135, and again as the motto of his essay on *Die Grundlage der Moral* (1840; included in *Die beiden Grundprobleme der Ethik,* 1841); Friedrich Nietzsche, *Schopenhauer als Erzieher* (1874), Section 7.

room; or we might consider emulating the Sophists by teaching students how to defend (or attack) *any* set of such judgments: we might resume the teaching of rhetoric. But the question remains whether the case for normative judgments can at best be persuasive and attractive and — returning to our central theme — whether a sound education can be based solely on a fusion of the analytical and historical approaches, while dispensing with any attempt to make normative judgments stick. This I do not believe.

Education Without Normative Judgments

Let us imagine an educational program (A) in which the analytical approach prevails and all the teachers guard against making normative judgments. They feel, let us say, that making such judgments without backing them up is illicit and an abuse of the teacher's privileged position, while backing them up is difficult if not impossible. The students in such a program would learn invaluable skills. They would be immune — in the optimal case — to many types of confusion and to much propaganda.

This immunity might be seriously compromised, however, if they had also been taught (B) that there are many types of language, including moral and religious language — perhaps even a language of Christianity, or even of Lutheranism, and in that case perhaps also a language of Marxism, or even of Stalinism. In that case, the analytically trained student might not be any more immune to propaganda or confusion than the historically trained students of German professors in the period between the two World Wars: the edge of criticism would be blunted by the apprehension that what seems confused or untenable makes perfectly good sense for those who have penetrated the alien idiom. As in philosophy seminars where texts are read in the original Greek and many students do not dare to criticize the authors because they are unsure of their own mastery of the language, analysts of *this* type are prone to suspend their critical powers.

In the case of either educational program (A as well as B), it would be pertinent to ask, Where would the students get their value judgments? Not from their scholarly teachers, presumably, but from people less inhibited by intellectual scruples. Having learned analytical techniques, the students might bring them to bear on some of the normative positions by which they had been brought up, possibly including in some cases the faith and morals of their parents, of preachers, of politicians, and of their own peer group. But if their teachers had all set a stern example of abstinence from value judgments, and in their analyses, too, had carefully avoided critical discussion of popular value judgments, preferring instead to concentrate on innocuous examples, of a mildly humorous nature whenever possible, then the students might well be inhibited by their intellectual conscience — or their academic superego — from dealing specifically and overtly with faith and morals. They would receive their faith and morals by osmosis (as practically everybody does) and eventually dispose of some of this material haphazardly if not unconsciously. In Socrates' sense, their lives would remain unexamined. To use the jargon of analytical philosophy, shouldn't we say that there was something odd about this?

In one sense, of course, it would not be odd at all, since "odd" often means uncommon, when what is common and ordinary is assumed as the norm. And of the situation just described one might well say, with Hamlet, "Ay, madam, it is common." But as this quotation reminds us, "common" and "ordinary" can also be terms of disparagement. In the jargon of analytical philosophy, "odd" signals that something is wrong, while being "ordinary" is considered a warrant of rightness, notwithstanding the connotation of "ornery." But in other contexts we sometimes feel that what is common and ordinary is, partly for that very reason, inferior. The value judgments we imbibe by osmosis, some of them through ordinary language, are not always free of confusion and mutual inconsistency.

In the case at hand, of course, our feeling that something would be odd about an education that led people to leave their lives unexamined would not be due to the fact that this occurrence is so common. Rather, it would be due to the fact that it is part of the rites of education in our liberal arts colleges to pay periodic lip service to Socrates' dictum that "the unexamined life is not worth living."

To eliminate such inconsistency, we might abandon Socrates' dictum and that whole tradition in the liberal arts, and especially in philosophy, which is rooted in it — or we could say that something was wrong with the kind of education just discussed. I embrace the second option: an education that does not lead students to examine their beliefs and normative judgments, especially those that influence their conduct and politics, has failed to that extent.

Is it possible to give reasons for this judgment? I might try to deduce it from value judgments you would grant me. But to be able to look for value judgments you would grant me, I should have to know who "you" are. For all I know, you may agree with my judgment even now — perhaps much more emphatically than you would agree with any higher-order value judgments from which I might try to deduce it. It is certainly not obvious that there is some one set of value judgments on which all who disagree with my lower-order judgment would agree.

What makes philosophy ridiculous to many minds is that philosophers often go out of their way to support popular positions that few would question, with abstruse arguments that few would accept. Even those who believe in God are perplexed by the ontological argument for his existence, and the point is even more obvious in ethics: the consensus on what is good and evil is far wider than agreement on the reasons philosophers have adduced for traditional moral judgments.

"Preaching morals is just as easy as giving reasons for morals is difficult." What is so difficult about it? Is it perhaps the fact that giving reasons does not help until one finds common ground — shared higher-order value judgments — and that this cannot be done in the abstract, once and for all, because common ground is shared by individuals or groups, and the search for common ground is therefore a subject for dialogue, not for a proof published in a journal? This way of putting it would give the false impression that reasons for normative judgments must differ radically from reasons for other judgments, as if at this point we had to abandon scientific procedure for mere rhetoric and attempts at persuasion. But in fact there are other alternatives to deduction besides Platonic dialogues and homiletic monologues, whether the latter are delivered from the pulpit or in existentialist tracts on authenticity.

Most contemporary philosophers have reached agreement on this point: the deductive model has no monopoly on rationality and intellectual respectability. Indeed, I expect that few philosophers or scholars in other fields would object to the following suggestion.

A CANON OF METHOD

The heart of scientific and rational procedure is this: Confronted with propositions, hypotheses, or views, we should ask what they mean; what considerations, evidence, and arguments support them; what speaks against them; what alternatives are available; and which of these is (or are) most plausible in the light of all this information.

One's audience and one's historical situation are always relevant when it comes to objections and alternatives. To have some imagination and the ability to invent objections and alternatives to one's own proposals is a virtue that can easily degenerate into a vice: disposing of a large number of objections and alternatives that have in fact never occurred to anybody soon becomes tedious and pointless. On the other hand, a responsible scholar must give some attention even to weak objections and untenable alternatives when these are widely accepted at the time.

Faced with an indefinite number of conceivable objections and alternatives, many of them easily disposed of, it is entirely rational to select for detailed attention the views of those to whom one addresses oneself, thus taking account of one's historical context and cultural environment. To ignore current orthodoxies would not be singularly rational but perverse.

This does not mean that we are justified in sharing the prejudices of our environment; on the contrary, it means that a scholar has a primary obligation to examine the orthodoxies of his own society and to be "the bad conscience" of his age. A searching critique of Sumerian or Aztec astronomy would not earn laurels for a twentieth century scientist: to win distinction one must score an advance over one's contemporaries.

This canon of method applies to normative judgments no less than to other propositions or views. Everything just said applies to them as well. But some explication of this canon may be helpful, and we shall proceed clause by clause. Only the first clause requires detailed discussion.

DIMENSIONS OF MEANING

The question of what a proposition, hypothesis, view, or value judgment means might seem to be the proper domain of analytical philosophy. But on reflection it appears that the historical approach also seeks an answer to this problem. And other approaches besides these two are relevant.

Indeed, "analytical philosophy" cannot be reduced to a single approach. At one time Wittgenstein suggested that "it was a good idea to ask oneself the question: How would one try to verify such an assertion?" But recalling this later on, he complained that "some people have turned this suggestion about asking for the verification into a dogma." [5] In those early days of the analytical movement it became a dogma that assertions not verifiable in principle were meaningless. Perhaps this stage of the movement should be distinguished from analytical philosophy proper and attributed to "the positivists." Thus Professor Pitcher has said in his book on *The Philosophy of Wittgenstein*:

The Positivists concluded from all this that in order for a proposition which is nontrivial (i.e., not a tautology or a contradiction) to be significant or meaningful—that is, to have a sense—there must be some observable conditions (states of affairs) whose existence

[5] D. A. T. G. (Gasking) and A. C. J. (Jackson), "Ludwig Wittgenstein," *The Australasian Journal of Philosophy*, Vol. XXIX, No. 2 (August, 1951), p. 79. The words cited are said to have come from remarks made by Wittgenstein at the Moral Sciences Club.

or non-existence would verify it. These conditions constitute its sense, and if there are no such conditions, it is devoid of sense (meaningless, nonsensical). So the criterion of the meaningfulness of a nontrivial proposition becomes, on this view, its verifiability, the possibility of verifying it. Metaphysical and ethical propositions, it was thought, obviously fail to satisfy this criterion.[6]

The later Wittgenstein suggested that the question of how one would verify an assertion was "just one way among others" and added, "For example, another question which is often very useful is to ask oneself: How is this word learnt? How would one set about teaching a child to use this word?"[7] And soon that suggestion was canonized, and the attempt to implement it has characterized much of analytical philosophy.

That both questions are useful and fruitful there is no denying, but they do not exhaust the meaning of a proposition. There are other dimensions of meaning, some of which may be spelled out here at least briefly.

First, we might speak of psychological meaning, referring to what a proposition, view, or value judgment means to the person who maintains it. This in turn is a complex matter, and under this heading we might therefore distinguish intended meaning (what a man is driving at or trying to say, though perhaps he puts his point badly, clumsily, misleadingly), emotional meaning (what it means to him in the sense in which it may mean a great deal to him and be heavy with associations), and perhaps also psychoanalytical meaning (assuming that an assertion may sometimes mean more to the speaker than he himself realizes).

It is possible to construe philosophy very narrowly, saying that all of this falls outside its province. But as long as a critic confines himself to the pros and cons of "what you said," ignoring what you were trying to say; as long, in other words, as he insists on being very literal and pays no heed to your intentions,

[6] George Pitcher, The Philosophy of Wittgenstein (Englewood Cliffs, N.J.: Prentice-Hall, Inc., 1964), pp. 166f.
[7] Gasking and Jackson, op. cit. For some discussion, see Walter Kaufmann, Critique of Religion and Philosophy (New York: Harper & Brothers, 1958; Doubleday Anchor Books, 1961), Section 19.

most people, including philosophers, would surely consider him either obtuse or captious and sophistical, and in both cases somewhat superficial. This is not to say that we should ever ignore what a person actually says or claims. But it is insufficient to dispose of what he said when he plainly did not mean to say quite what he did say. And there is no need to stipulate that only obtuse or captious criticism is truly philosophical.

So much may be granted by some philosophers who would nevertheless wish to draw the line this side of emotional meaning. After all, those positivists who claimed that such statements as, for example, "God exists" or "murder is evil" were "meaningless" never meant to deny that such statements might be rich in emotional meaning. (This shows incidentally how important it is, even in discussing the logical positivists, to distinguish what they often said from their intended meaning.) But will it really do for philosophers to ignore emotional meaning altogether? In many cases it certainly will do, but in some very interesting cases it may be impossible to determine the intended meaning without considering the emotional meaning. The proposition "God exists" is a case in point, and the lasting importance of John Wisdom's essay "Gods" [8] is largely due to the fact that he called attention to this.

Delving into the supposed psychoanalytical meaning of a proposition or view is probably not advisable for philosophers in most cases because any claims about such meanings are usually so uncertain and disputable. But it is worth noting that we are confronted with a continuum that extends from overt meanings to intended meanings, which sometimes cannot be understood unless we consider emotional meanings, which in turn may remain puzzling and unclear and invite attempts to descend yet further' to unconscious roots. So much for psychological meaning.

One also might consider sociological meaning and historical meaning, even though most philosophers may be ill equipped

[8] *Proceedings of the Aristotelian Society,* 1944–45; often reprinted, e.g., in *Logic and Language,* ed. Antony Flew (New York: Doubleday Anchor Books, 1965), and Walter Kaufmann, *Religion from Tolstoy to Camus* (New York: Harper Torchbooks, 1964).

to deal with these dimensions. After all, some philosophers may be very good indeed in doing research of this kind; and if it is done well it often supplements philosophical analysis in the narrower sense in a very illuminating manner, regardless of the academic department to which the investigator happens to belong. In the case of history this point is purely obvious, and it is widely taken for granted — quite rightly — that for certain kinds of philosophical work a philosopher has to master some of the skills of the historian. Without that he cannot hope to do justice to Aristotle's or Spinoza's meaning.

Instead of going on to philological meaning and trying to make a list of as many dimensions of meaning as possible, let us be satisfied with just one more type of meaning that is pre-eminently part of a philosopher's concern: the ramifications of a view must be explored to spell out its meaning.

The meaning of an action or policy is clearly not confined to its intention, its emotional charge, its unconscious motivation, or even its historical or sociological context; it also consists of its probable and actual consequences and its relation to other actions or policies. The same is true of the meaning of at least some propositions and views. If there is one type of meaning that is more specifically philosophical than any other, I should opt for this dimension of meaning.

Human sacrifices or prayers, for example, can be analyzed in many ways to explicate their meaning, or their many possible meanings. Some such analyses are pre-eminently psychological or historical, or possibly philological or sociological, which is not at all to say that they are philosophically irrelevant or uninteresting. But what if not philosophical should one call an analysis of the meaning of prayer or human sacrifices in terms of their implications? What would a god have to be like if he stopped the cruel suffering of a child if, and only if, offered a human sacrifice, or if a group of people got down on their knees to beg him and praise him? And what, if any, answer would those who perform sacrifices, or who pray, give to this question?

This example is somewhat explosive and cracks the confines of its immediate context. It shows how analysis and "normative philosophy" are far from being mutually exclusive. Often the analysis of implications constitutes the crucial part of giving reasons for or against a value judgment. Strictly speaking, this analysis is only a preliminary step, part of the attempt to determine meanings; but very often there is sufficient agreement about higher-level value judgments to make it almost unnecessary to spell out the final deduction explicitly, though it is possible at that point to call into question the higher-order value judgment, as theologians do occasionally when it turns out to entail impious conclusions.

Such analysis as is here recommended is different from the type Wittgenstein recommended. After all, he insisted that philosophy "leaves everything as it is." [9] The kind of analysis recommended here, like that practiced by Socrates, can come into conflict with the faith and morals of the age. And it is not concerned primarily with language; the analysis is not primarily linguistic. Rather, one explores the ramifications of a view, both logical and practical, to determine what it means.

Pros, Cons, Alternatives, and Decision

Once the meaning of a view has been determined, we should ask what considerations, evidence, and arguments support it, and what speaks against it. This goes both for value judgments (say, about prayer) and alleged assertions of fact (say, about the character of God or the exact date of some historical event). Of course, the nature of relevant evidence and arguments will differ from case to case, depending on the type of the claim: one does not argue about historical statements the way one argues about generalizations.

Is the case altogether different when it comes to normative judgments? Here appeal must be made occasionally to higher-order value judgments; but often these higher-order judgments are not controversial. If they are called into question, they in turn have to be treated in accordance with our canon. If in this

[9] Ludwig Wittgenstein, *Philosophical Investigations,* trans. G. E. M. Anscombe (New York: The Macmillan Co., 1953), Section 124.

process higher and higher echelons of normative judgments should be reached and disagreement about norms should persist until the very end, this would be most unusual; in almost all cases disagreement about normative judgments is reducible to disagreements about facts or probabilities, which is not to say that such disagreements can always be resolved. But even in the exceptional case in which no common norms are reached, a great deal of clarification would be achieved about the interrelation of value judgments, about the relevance of various kinds of information, and about precisely what is involved in each position and in the disagreement.

There are some who are impressed by an array of supporting quotations or evidence without asking about negative evidence and counter-arguments, or about alternative hypotheses that might fare at least as well if not better. This is a common fault not only among students but also among bad scientists, historians, and theologians. A historian who disregards negative evidence and alternative hypotheses is, to that extent, a bad historian. In theology, on the other hand, the disregard of equally plausible alternatives — or rather, no less implausible alternatives — is part of the rules of the game; and for that reason among others, theology, far from being the queen of the sciences, is basically unscientific.[10]

Some "normative philosophers" — or, to speak more idiomatically, some moral philosophers, estheticians, and political philosophers — resemble theologians rather than good scientists and historians. But there is no reason why philosophers in these fields who do not eschew value judgments *must* defy our canon. On the contrary, they need not confine themselves to objections actually offered by their contemporaries; they can go out of their way to consider a few particularly powerful objections that have not occurred to anybody else. And they certainly can go on to examine alternatives.

The notion that normative judgments differ fundamentally at

[10] See Walter Kaufmann, *Critique of Religion and Philosophy*, op. cit., Chapter VI, and *The Faith of a Heretic*, op. cit., Chapter V.

this point from hypotheses about matters of fact is due, at least in large part, to a crucial error. Many people suppose that one must choose between two views which are in fact both untenable: either, they suppose, all views, hypotheses, and value judgments are equally sound and respectable, or, whenever alternatives are available, only one of these is tenable. In fact, it is palpable that many hypotheses and normative positions are confused, self-contradictory, at odds with relevant evidence, and altogether untenable; but in some cases two or more positions are equally plausible. The incidence of such cases may well be higher in the normative field, and in some instances more rival positions may be equally plausible than is generally the case in the sciences; but if this should be so, the difference would be one of degree and not one of principle. What matters in ethics and other areas of philosophy where attempts are sometimes made to work out normative positions is, as in the sciences and in history, that the position is worked out carefully and in detail, and that due weight is given to our canon.

It may seem that this could be done in theology no less than in ethics, whether theologians have been doing it in fact or not. I have tried to show elsewhere[11] that the rules of the game in theology are such that the construction of alternative systems is easy to the point of pointlessness, and that these rules are fundamentally different from the rules that are acknowledged by scientists and historians. To put the matter differently and a little more kindly: theology is essentially homiletic; normative philosophy need not be homiletic and often is not.

The main job of normative philosophy is, as I see it, to work out tenable positions, giving due weight to supporting considerations, objections, and alternatives. Where that can be done, one should show why one position appears to be more plausible than any other that seems to be available. If two or more positions should appear to be more or less equally tenable, one should give one's reasons for preferring one or for not preferring any.

[11] *Ibid.*

A Critique of Value-Free Education

We are now ready to take another look at education without normative judgments. We considered it briefly before, more or less as a thought experiment, by imagining an educational program in which the analytical approach prevailed and the teachers guarded against making normative judgments, and we suggested that in that case most of the students would never be led to examine their lives in the Socratic sense. I then said that an education that does not lead students to examine their beliefs and their normative judgments has failed to that extent. And then we raised the question of whether this judgment could be supported by good reasons, which in turn led us to propose and explicate a canon of method. Now let us return once more to education without normative judgments, not just as a thought experiment.

Higher education in the United States and in many other countries limps on both legs. It is certainly not entirely "value-free," to use the suggestive term introduced by Max Weber in his plea for value-free science; but the realm of facts is still widely considered the proper domain of reason and scientific procedures, while value judgments and commitments are held to be rooted in man's irrational nature and hence beyond rational discussion.[12] This is the common ground of those on the one hand who consider facts respectable and value judgments "merely" emotive and not cognitive, and those on the other hand who find ultimate commitments deeper than "merely" scientific discourse. Both tend to rule out rational discussion of questions involving value judgments.

Great scholars are often attracted to this position. A man who has done much research finds it difficult to communicate even a fraction of his scholarship to his students and is therefore glad to leave value questions to preachers and less scholarly

[12] The classical statement is still Max Weber's *Wissenschaft als Beruf* (1919). For a detailed rebuttal, see Walter Kaufmann, "Ketzerei in der Erziehung," *Club Voltaire*, Vol. II (1965), pp. 303–314.

teachers who may prefer an inspirational approach. Beset by an excess of data and discoveries, he regrets that he has to omit so much, looks down on teachers who do not suffer from the same embarrassment of riches, and questions whether they belong on the faculty of a great university.

As a result, questions of life and death for individuals, for society, and even for mankind rarely receive the kind of careful and conscientious discussion that is lavished on many far less important problems. Vital decisions tend to be surrendered to emotion, impulse, and dogmatism — or to men who *claim* to have the answers.

Historically, this has been the price professors have paid for academic freedom: leave us alone, they said in effect to governments, churches, and alumni, and we shall confine our attention to matters of no vital concern to you. (In Germany, moreover, where "the modern conception of academic freedom came to be formulated" during the nineteenth century,[13] professors, being civil servants, were sometimes held not to have the right to criticize their government.) But American professors often complain that their students conform too much, are too anxious to be liked, too afraid to stick out their necks, and too lacking in political concerns. The faculty sees how the worry about election to clubs and fraternities stimulates a deadening conformity and a concern for popularity that are unworthy of educated men. But the faculty often fails to note how the same vices are bred in its own ranks:

Graduate students who need their professors to recommend them for good jobs are concerned not to antagonize their teachers or the men who might hire them, and the Ph.D. thesis, which sets the pattern for subsequent scholarly publications, is not designed to encourage young professors-to-be to stick out their necks. What is wanted is something solid and safe. Having got his first job, the young man is under pressure to write a few

[13] Ralph F. Fuchs, "Academic Freedom—Its Basic Philosophy, Function, and History," in *Academic Freedom*, ed. Hans W. Baade and R. O. Everett (Dobbs Ferry, N.Y.: Oceana Publications, Inc., 1964), p. 5. Most of the twelve essays in this volume are richly footnoted and open up the literature on academic freedom.

articles for professional journals, and again the same considerations apply. Occasionally a young scholar publishes something bold, but the pressures of his training and career militate against this. While they strive for permanent tenure young professors rarely avail themselves of the academic freedom they have; and when they get permanent positions the pattern is usually set. The refusal to deal with normative questions must be seen in this perspective, too.

History and sociology can thus help us to understand the position we want to attack. Moreover, it is surely right that professors should not abuse their privileged positions to pontificate about matters beyond their special competence; students take courses to learn about the subject, not to listen to homilies. Nevertheless the view that value judgments have no place in higher education and should be offered with apologies, if at all, is vitiated by three profound errors.

First, persuasion is usually much more effective when one does not state one's valuations openly. To convert his students to his value judgments, a professor should find it much easier to select and present the facts in his own way, leaving the final verdict to his students. That way they may congratulate themselves on their good judgment when in fact they are adopting his. The teacher who openly states his own value judgments, supports them with reasons as best he can, and frankly acknowledges uncomfortable facts, objections, and alternatives gives a splendid example of honesty.

Secondly, it is unfortunately quite false that students trained by great scholars generally learn on their own to apply to morals, politics, and other vital issues the critical thinking they have been taught to apply to academic questions. During the first third of this century the German universities could boast of a galaxy of distinguished scholars who applied the highest standards in their specialties and won a large number of Nobel Prizes. But their students did not learn to apply similar standards of rationality to moral and political questions, and Hitler was as popular with students and university-trained people as with less educated Germans.

Third, the dichotomy of fact and value is misleading. To begin from the side of fact, the selection of subject matter — to whom or what we devote a whole course, how much time is spent on this and that, what and who is read, and what is slighted or left out altogether — involves value judgments at every turn. Our teaching and writing are shot through with value judgments. We should bring these out into the open and examine them.

What is wrong with the dichotomy of fact and value can also be seen by considering value judgments. They are rarely independent of what we take to be facts. Is X a good president? Is Y a good policy? Was intervention justified? Was this action wicked? One of the most important parts of education is to learn to analyze such questions, to determine what information is relevant and how to get and use it. It is also important to discuss which, if any, of one's value judgments one would be willing to maintain regardless of all consequences.

Alas, professors who want to, and have to, cover a lot of subject matter usually cannot take the time to concentrate attention on some of their value judgments, analyzing their precise meaning, examining the pros and cons, and comparing them with alternatives. It might therefore seem that my suggestions are at best very nice but unfortunately impractical.

A Modest Proposal for Faculty Forums

Let me therefore conclude with a specific proposal. I want to recommend an innovation in higher education. Our universities should institute faculty forums — regular occasions when two or three professors who do not agree discuss important questions before any interested colleagues and students, not in an attempt to score points but to give an example of responsible investigation.

Too many administrators suppose that academic education must consist of courses, and that the proper fusion of breadth and depth must be a function of requirements. Even now, however, guest lectures and panel discussions are often remembered decades after most course work has been forgotten. Yet most panels are too large because those organizing them are more fearful of a moment's thoughtful silence than of the impossibility of ever exploring any problem more than superficially. More than three panelists are almost always too many. And since the speakers are almost always outsiders, not members of the regular faculty, the vicious bifurcation of academic education and real life is reinforced.

Moreover, as professors gain distinction they become less available to students. Men who want to get on with important research which immediately benefits their own teaching and, after publication, also teachers and students at other institutions, cannot be burdened with heavy teaching schedules and one small discussion group after another: threatened with that, they would go elsewhere. Many teach only a couple of advanced courses and are thus utterly beyond the reach of almost all students. As a result, more and more students are bitterly disappointed by the great universities they attend. Forums would make it possible for interested students to hear many of their most eminent professors not only lecture but also question each other and, after that, respond to questions from the audience. These forums would create some sense of a community of scholars: the students would see their teachers as human beings who struggle with vital problems.

Our society desperately needs vigorous and informed discussion of many questions involving valuations. Where should such discussion develop if not at our universities? Those who drafted the Constitution of the United States thought of the Senate. But even senators whose education and intelligence fits them for such discussion must think of re-election. In the executive branch of our government highly informed discussion of specific issues takes place, but behind closed doors, and there is a tendency to rely on those, listen to those, and discuss with those on whose basic agreement one can rely; whoever is in *basic* disagreement tends to resign or to be fired. And we need responsible discussion not only of day-to-day issues but also of goals and principles.

Few professors are eager to take on this burden. Signing statements written by committees, making occasional declarations of faith by way of standing up to be counted, and even marching and picketing take less time and seem more dramatic. The old notion that where values are at stake emotion must take over does not die easily.

Specialized scholarship, however, is the best way to acquire high standards of evidence and careful thinking. Having acquired such standards and the techniques to satisfy them, scholars can make major contributions by bringing them to bear on questions concerned with punishment, civil disobedience, foreign policy, and faith and morals. Scholars obviously should not forsake their specialties; but instead of discouraging them from occasionally speaking out on such matters, after taking time to prepare themselves, we should provide regular forums for them — not to pontificate but to discuss.

To what extent do different value judgments and systems depend on different beliefs about facts and probabilities, and to what extent are different ends desired, and why? To say simply that different goals are rooted in different commitments is rarely helpful or profound; rational discussion can determine much more than that.

It is not surprising that our social needs and our educational needs should converge. The central question of the philosophy of education is: What kinds of men and women should we try to develop? This was very clearly understood by Plato. And though I do not accept his answer to this question, he also understood that types of men are corollaries of types of societies, or vice versa. If you want to produce "organization men" and the kind of society that breeds them, you will not want faculty forums. A philosophy of education is centered in a vision of what might be made of man and society. I want a society in which the merits of different types can be examined and compared. I want men and women who try to be rational about life's most important decisions. Our present education is not nearly as good as it might be. I should not be surprised if all the speakers agreed on this, and to the extent to which we try to back up such an estimate we all speak "from the point of view of a normative philosophy."

Chapter 3 / *The Contribution of Philosophy of the Social Sciences to Educational Development*

MICHAEL SCRIVEN

INTRODUCTION

Education is an applied social science, although it is probably the most misapplied and least scientific of the social sciences. If the philosophy of the social sciences has anything useful to say to the applied social sciences, it certainly should have something to say to the educator, the educational psychologist, and perhaps the philosopher of education. Whether or not it has anything useful to say *to* them, it certainly should have something to say *about* them, for the philosopher of science should certainly discuss the nature of applied social sciences.

My own interests are very much in the applications of the philosophy of science, and I think the interesting applications here can probably be best found by a direct attack on the philosophical aspects of the specific problem the educator faces. But it is important to remember that practical suggestions may also occur as by-products of the entirely legitimate subject of *pure* philosophy of science, the task of which is the analysis of the nature of science without directly aiming at improvement in the practice of science. This subject corresponds to pure mathematics and, like pure mathematics, the fact that it sometimes *incidentally* comes up with valuable practical results means that it may still be defensible in terms of pay-off, even though it is not aimed at pay-off. Its aim is to meet the purely intellectual challenge of analyzing what exists. In this short essay, I shall be mainly concerned with rather specific and practical suggestions, but they as often arise from consideration of general philosophical issues as from attempts to handle the difficulties the practitioner faces. Whether the original *motive* for their development is pure or applied research, then, a number of results in the philosophy of the social sciences have practical consequences for education.

Another feature of the topic which I find attractive, besides its practical orientation, is that no one can say what it excludes. I shall construe philosophy of the social sciences very broadly, as I believe it can most usefully be construed. In this sense it must include certain elements common to the philosophy of any kind of science, such as the theory of scientific definition, the theory of testability (to which pertains discussion of operationism and the verification principle), the theory of taxonomies, discussion of reductionism-holism, explanation-prediction theory, theories about probability and scientific inference, and so on. Some of these topics have special twists for the social sciences; explanation-theory must cope with the insight and *verstehen* approaches, prediction-theory with the free-will issue. And there are other philosophical or logical problems, or aspects of the preceding problems, which are even more specific to the social sciences, such as the facts/values debate (manifesting itself in the problem of interpersonal comparison of utilities in economics and in political philosophy, for example), the introspection *vs.* observation dispute, the problem of providing an over-all assessment of the social sciences' view of man, and the problem of the relationship between the social sciences and other subjects.

The problem here and now is simply one of selection. I find every one of these topics extremely interesting, and I have even thought (certainly insufficiently) and published (probably excessively) about each of them. As a criterion for selection, I am going to construe the term "educational development" in the title of the conference on which this book is based, and of this chapter, rather precisely (although I take "social sciences" to include history and environmental medicine). I take educational development to be the goal of the education of the individual, to which I take the contribution of the social sciences to be direct and indirect: direct, in that some knowledge of the philosophy of the social sciences should be part of, or a mark of, educational development, and indirect, in that some issues in the philosophy of the social sciences essentially control — through the sub-topics mentioned in the last paragraph — the structure and the contents of substantial parts of the ordinary curriculum.

Even with this preliminary focusing, the subject is too extensive, and I shall consider only a small part of it. I shall discuss the way in which the *methodology* of the social sciences is distinctive and should be directly incorporated in any curriculum aimed at educational development, and indirectly accepted in any teaching or testing procedures we use. In connection with this I shall say something very briefly about the incorporation of value-analysis and value criteria in the curriculum. And I shall say something about one of the *conclusions* of philosophy of the social sciences, about the conception of man that emerges from the social sciences, which should surely be part of any educational core we build into our curricula. In general, one might say, the *spirit* that the philosophy of the social sciences must try to convey throughout the process of educational development is the spirit of critical scrutiny of the scrutineer, for these are the subjects whose subject-matter is the student.

The Methodology of the Social Sciences and Education Today

The social sciences are chiefly responsible for the most significant advances in scientific method since the origin of modern physics, but only a tiny percentage of the school population learns anything about them. Moreover, these methods are easily taught, are of very great value in everyday life, and are practically essential in almost every professional field. I am thinking of the principles of experimental design that are exhibited in double-blind studies, or in the use of matched control groups, in the identification of significant correlations, in scaling and measuring methodology, in the empirical validation of tests, in inter-judge or test-retest consistency checks, in sampling and stratification procedures, or in a dozen other aspects of standard methodology in the social sciences. These are the methods which have enabled us to conquer the problem of studying ourselves scientifically, and yet they are so imperfectly understood that serious discussions continue at the faculty level on whether psychology is or can be a "real science." It not only is a science, it is the paradigm science, whereas classical physics or astronomy is the special case — the lucky special case. What makes a subject scientific is not spectacular or simple results but the method of approach. The simple methods of the early forms of physics, or even the complex *technology* of contemporary research tools in physics, are not as sophisticated, methodologically, as the smoking–lung-cancer studies or the experimental designs for good educational- or psychotherapy-outcome research. It is certainly true that the quantity of results from such studies is still quite limited, but there are plenty of fully objective results from simpler studies, and we have the tools for the big jobs, if not yet the financial fuel to run them.

The overdue revolution in the content of education is the revolution in teaching students how to think about human behavior. We are in the peak period of a revolution designed to put highly organized and truly insightful physical science, and even biological science and mathematics, into the curriculum. But we are in a period when what is needed is no longer this but a better capacity to think about human affairs scientifically. The pressure of Sputnik may turn out to have given us a push in the wrong direction, but not for the usual reason — not because it has led us to neglect the humanities. The humanities have been around a long time but have shown little sign of generating humanity. The social sciences have been around long enough to develop a method which, though it will not guarantee an improvement in the humaneness of our responses, may at least guarantee an improvement in their rationality. And we may hope there is some correlation between rationality and humanity.

Not that the social sciences have sorted out all the methodological problems that they have faced. Indeed they are even markedly deficient in the application of the techniques already available to the problems that face society. The fields of psychotherapy and education stand untilled by the heavy plows that are required to make them yield the crop we seek. But even if the social sciences are by no means developed fully, they *are* developed far enough to improve the level of our thinking on most of the subjects which require our decision, and all of the subjects on which the fate of the nation can be said to hinge. At the personal level, the defensive response to the smoking–lung-cancer studies has demonstrated to the social scientist the thinness of the veneer of rationality in such matters. A thorough education in the principles of experimental design and investigation, such as that possessed by the chief investigators, almost invariably led to the abandonment of heavy cigarette smoking. It was not just their exposure to the horrific pictures of cancerous lungs, but their realization of the total failure of picayune attempts at counter-arguments. For a live demonstration of the failure of college education, one has only to listen to the discussions of the statistics by representatives of the advertising agencies managing the big cigarette accounts. And for a demonstration of the failure of our society to develop education as a science, one has only to listen to the discussions, even among teachers, of comparative methods of teaching and grading. Teaching is an art that at least should be based upon science — but often has no connection with it. The general level of discussion of the actual merits of the new math curricula or the new physics curricula or the new biology curricula can only be described as primitive. Representatives of the government office supporting educational research are full of such jolly catch-phrases as "Evaluation is impossible — we don't know what to evaluate for, and even if we did, we wouldn't know how to do it." We stand in the middle of the most gigantic educational extravaganza in history, and we find ourselves asking what is the show *for?* If it is for the education of citizens, it does a staggeringly inefficient job in the dimensions of the greatest need. If it is for the education, the edification, or even the emolument of scholars, the situation is worse. Indeed, it is only if one views the educational apparatus as a device to keep creative teachers and textbook writers from death by frustration that one can see it as even modestly efficient.

Well, the tools for reform lie at hand. If we are fortunate enough to have time to employ them, before the holocaust, then reform must be wrought by education, in particular by improving our education for the capacity to think about our education. And that means education in the methods of the social sciences. The citizen needs it today, the scholar needs it today, the businessman needs it, and the school administrator needs it. But I do not know of a single course on the methods of the social sciences in a single high school in this country, and I know of very few courses in the social sciences in which any kind of generalization of the particular methods discussed is stressed. This is much less true, but still distressingly true, at the college level.

THE SIGNIFICANCE OF THE SOCIAL SCIENCES

The educational importance of the social sciences arises from the fact that the social sciences provide us with tools for analytical thinking about matters of common and technical concern. But their significance goes deeper than this. Their significance lies in the fact that they represent the scientific triumph over the last barrier to scientific progress.

With the work by Harvey on the circulation of the blood a tremendous stride forward was made in the study of the human organism. The subsequent development of embryology, histology, pathology, and physiology has advanced the study of man as a material mechanism impressively. But no one ever felt that the circulation of the blood was part of the distinctive, essential nature of man — part of the set of properties whose combination distinguishes him from lower organisms. The development of the theory of evolution drove one spike into the doctrine of the supernatural nature of man by showing that his development could be regarded as simply one example of a natural process leading to more highly specialized organisms from a beginning in primordial slimes or prebiotic stews. It was still possible, however, to maintain that the soul was "breathed into" man's ancestral strain at some point in its development. And it was still all too easily possible to be impressed by the differences between man and the less highly developed animals. If one *was* thus impressed, the possibility of belief in the *essentially different* nature of man remained. With the Cartesian doctrine that animals were mere automata — a doctrine which made the early days of vivisection much easier, and which therefore contributed substantially to medical progress — we found a philosopher reinforcing doctrines which were characteristic of theologians and hence of most thinking. If man was essentially different, perhaps in alone possessing a mind composed of (or residing in) some essentially different substance from that of the body, then it was indeed plausible to imagine that the study of man might suffer from limitations which more and more obviously did not hamper the study of physical phenomena.

And so we come to the period when the scientific social sciences begin. With the awkward and indeed largely unsuccessful beginnings of experimental psychology and the initially more successful beginnings of sociology, with the increasing development of work in comparative cultural anthropology, and to a much lesser extent with the development of models of economic man, the last barrier began to crumble. The intervening years have seen many hard-won battles at this last barrier, and the years to come will see more, but we have now finally won our way to the last foothold which we need to carry the war and complete the conquest. Whether we shall succeed in holding this position against the forces of reaction is another question, but I believe that we have now solved the last intellectual problem in the way of scientific social science. The subject which I think has given us the key to this solution is the study of computers and computer simulation of human processes. Although it is important to see with Darwin that the human being probably evolved in the same way as other living organisms, this does not show that he did not evolve into a crucially different kind of entity. But he did not. He is a superior animal among the animals, but he is not a creature of a different kind, the only owner of a mind. The demonstration that a mechanical entity can compete successfully with a human, not only in speed of calculation, but — as it now begins to appear — in every respect in which a human skill or sensibility can be defined, produces an ultimate humility comparable to that involved in the discovery that our planet is simply one among many, rather than being the center of the universe. Of course, parity of performance by a super-computer does not demonstrate that we are super-computers. But it places any alternative hypothesis on the defensive, and at present it appears that no alternative hypothesis is defensible. To say all this is not to say that there are no significant differences between men and machines or between men and animals. It is only to say that these differences are matters of degree and of the direction of specialization and of the particular combination of properties that distinguishes man, rather than a matter of the possession of substances or skills that are essentially different from those of mechanisms or monkeys.

This final recognition of the truth of mechanism or materialism is no ground for supposing that the cruder inferences that have often been thought to follow from this doctrine are valid. In particular, it is no ground for supposing that the mind does not "really" exist, or that it lacks efficacy, or that man has no moral or aesthetic sense. To stress the point again, it is no ground for supposing that man is not importantly and interestingly different from presently known animal forms and probably from all future ones — and different indeed from presently existing computers and in all probability from future super-computers. But these differences can now be seen as simply reflecting different environmental pressures, and the consequent different emphasis on specializations in different directions. The mental life and language of homo sapiens is indeed richer than that of any other entity we know of or can construct at the moment, but then the richness of mental life is not a difference of kind. Other organisms feel pain and have memories, and artificial entities can be made that will also feel pain and remember in the same sense as man.

Although, in this essay, I am not fully substantiating these claims about the nature of man,[1] they still need substantiation, for they have been hotly debated in recent years as in each one of the last two thousand. Still, I believe that genuinely original arguments and data have come to light in recent years which have tipped the balance in favor of the materialistic approach (though perhaps, because of some of the associations it has acquired, that word makes one so nervous that it would be better to use the term "physicalistic"). My task is to draw the conclusions that I think are appropriate for education from what I take to be the philosophical implications of the social sciences, rather than to establish those implications against all possible objections. But it is appropriate to consider one or two of the most important objections, because they too should be discussed in the educational process. Indeed, it would be quite inappropriate to recommend the dogmatic indoctrination of students with the point of view I have just put forward, just as it is quite inappropriate to dogmatically indoctrinate them with views about the superiority of free enterprise and the immorality of socialism, or the reverse. The good teacher is supposed to be a leader, not a brainwasher. Good teaching about the nature of man requires that the position just described be presented and discussed most thoroughly, which is certainly not the case at the moment. Whether or not it can now be thought of as the consensus of social and biological scientists is unimportant; the question is whether or not it is now an important contender for the title of the correct view of man.

In this society there is far too much commitment to the propriety of the cruder religious views about the nature of man: for example, the view that he is divine in nature, that he transcends determinism, that he will live beyond the grave, etc. This commitment is, I fear, far more a product of a reaction against the doctrine of materialism held by our political opponents than

---

[1] I have tried to do so in the chapter entitled "Man" in *Primary Philosophy* (New York: McGraw-Hill Book Co., Inc., 1966).

the product of our independent and well-confirmed thinking. At any rate, such positions are without rational foundations, in my view, and they represent a point of view which should be recognized as incompatible in spirit with the scientific one. One of the most popular myths in the intellectual sub-culture of this society is the one about the essential compatibility of science and religion. This compatibility exists as long as religion has nothing to say about the nature of man other than a phenomenological description of what man thinks of as religious experience, or a metaphorical account of his moral problems. In this same sense science is compatible with aesthetic experiences and the discussion of them by artists and critics. But religion never rests content with this meager portion; it never has, and, I expect, never will. And every inch that religion goes beyond this tree-trimming role is an inch which must be won back from the minds of those who are indoctrinated in religious schools or religious homes or churches, won back not only in the classroom but in the lawcourts and the legislatures. Every suggestion that man has a spiritual nature which is essentially supernatural, every suggestion that moral questions are best settled by referral to divine commandment, ancient writ, or holy revelation is educationally pernicious and socially dangerous. It is educationally pernicious because it is not well founded, and because it leads to a tendency to withhold our strictest scrutiny from ourselves, and it is socially dangerous because the effect of that attitude is to make possible the belief that we have some kind of divine sanction for our actions that renders them justifiable, even when no justification can be given in terms of the welfare on this earth, in this life, of those whom we affect. Let us look more closely at some of these issues, especially two that bear on questions of methodology as well as substance.

The Understanding of Human Behavior

Of the few topics that I shall be able to discuss in the space available, I select this and place it first because of the important *indirect* consequences it has for education in the social studies, especially history. The problem of the kind of understanding that we can expect to have of human beings has often been answered in a way that suggests that we cannot have the usual kind of scientific understanding of them, or that the scientific understanding we can have is very much less than all that we should demand. So this dispute, which is a dispute in the philosophy of the social sciences, is also a dispute about what kind of material should be contained in history textbooks and what kind of questions should be asked in history classrooms — or in classrooms in which sociology or anthropology or economics or psychopathology are discussed at all. And, of course, it is closely connected with questions about whether man is essentially different from other objects in the universe.

The claim has been made that with respect to the behavior of other human beings we have available to us a kind of insight, a type of understanding, which is different in kind from that provided by the ordinary kind of explanation in the physical sciences. This insight or understanding is sometimes referred to as empathic, sometimes (the two are not generally accepted as interchangeable) as *verstehen*. Supporters of Weber and Collingwood sometimes talk about "seeing actions from the inside," i.e., seeing them as they appear to the agent, as the essential part of understanding them, and as being something which is not possible if we merely subsume the event or action under a general law in the way that is thought to be characteristic of ordinary scientific explanation. Sometimes the claims for this independent method of understanding are further supported by the denial of the possibility of the other kind, in connection with human affairs, often on the grounds that we simply lack general laws of any kind of precision.

From the point of view which I am expounding rather than defending here, I want to make two quite different kinds of comment on the *verstehen* view. On the one hand, it seems clear to me that this kind of understanding is an entirely appropriate and legitimate kind. On the other hand, it is quite inappropriate to regard it as involving some special kind of insight or sense that goes beyond the scientific framework. So I wish to support the *verstehen* theorists in one important claim or group of claims that they make, while denying the legitimacy of further claims that are often made by such theorists. As I see it, the solution of this issue depends upon making a point which is not commonly made and denying a point which is commonly made. To begin with the denial, the picture of scientific explanation which is painted by opponents of the *verstehen* theorists seems to me quite certainly false. It is grossly oversimplified, and in recent years has come under fire from a number of independent sources and with respect to every single one of its claims.

Explanation, and in particular scientific explanation, is a chameleon creature, and subsumption under a general law of the kind that is said to be required is most certainly not a universal characteristic of it. The key feature of scientific explanation is the production of understanding; this often amounts to the reduction of the incomprehensible to the comprehensible. We try to exhibit the behavior of light, or sound, or liquid helium as analogous to the behavior of particles, of elastic transmission phenomena, or of a hitherto unknown combination of two substances with relatively well-understood properties. The old account of explanation as reduction to the familiar is a special case of this kind of maneuver, but it is misleadingly phrased, for the familiar is not always understood, and what is understood is not just the familiar. Reduction to the comprehensible is the right catch-phrase, if one must have one.

The common account of scientific explanation as subsumption under general laws is again a special case of the correct general account. If we understand the general law under which we subsume the phenomenon, then this *is* a case of reduction to the comprehensible. But there are many occasions when subsumption under a general law provides no understanding whatsoever; indeed, it deepens the lack of understanding by showing that it applies to a wider range of phenomena than was at first supposed, and hence no explanation takes place. One cannot normally expect to *explain* the fact that light obeys Snell's Law by saying that all electromagnetic radiation does so. Furthermore, just as subsumption is not always explanatory, there are many other ways of explaining a phenomenon than by subsumption under a universal law. One may, for example, come to understand how a machine works by a discussion with a mechanic who points out the way in which one gear wheel moves another gear wheel, is controlled by a centrifugal governor, etc. To understand this operation is not to see it as an example of some general law about machines of this kind, or even a combination of general laws about parts of machines of this kind; it is to see the whole as comprehensible because it consists of parts whose relationship is comprehensible. The comprehensibility of the way in which the parts work is not a matter of their operating in a way in which all such parts work, though no doubt there is some class of mechanical parts such that all its members do act in this way. For that merely generalizes the phenomenon under study. It is to see that torque, applied to this gear wheel in a clockwise direction, will necessarily move the circumference of the inter-meshed gear wheel in a counter-clockwise direction, and how the governor controls speed, and so on. This is understood perfectly by self-taught African mechanics with no knowledge of the underlying physical laws. So comprehension is not a matter of knowing the deeper physical analysis. Nor is it just a matter of getting used to the way things are, for no matter how used we get to the fact that injections of a certain chemical produce phenomenal healing of radiation burns, this will not make the healing comprehensible. The notion of comprehensibility is quite a difficult matter. But it frequently involves the analysis of something into simpler components, the analysis consisting of exhibiting the relation between the components. Actually, the truth is rather messier, as appears when one attacks the meaning of "simpler"; one must say that explaining something is always done in a context in which it can be assumed that other things, phenomena and relations, are not in need of explanation because they are already understood. Explaining consists of exhibiting the not-understood as a combination, of an understood kind, of understood components.

Now this notion of the reduction of a phenomenon into acceptable components is very closely connected, where the concept of a model is relevant, to perception of the phenomenon in terms of a familiar, i.e., understood, model. The crucial point about a model is that it has familiar component parts, and the relationships between these parts are understood. (I am not using the term "model" in the sense in which it is over-extended to include mere mathematical descriptions.) The proposal that I have to make about the relevance of all this to the social sciences is as follows: The *verstehen* approach represents the use of a particular kind of model for explanation, namely the model of the human being himself. This is indeed a special kind of model — and in that sense different from those models appropriate to an explanation of physical phenomena — but it is also a perfectly standard kind, and the procedure of explaining behavior in terms of this comprehended model is perfectly scientific. To be more specific, it would be necessary to go into a rather elaborate account of the nature of understanding. An important indicator of understanding certain phenomena is the capacity to anticipate the future behavior of what is understood, although this is not a necessary condition for understanding. For understanding to be non-vacuous, certain possibilities must be excluded by the model that is thought to provide the understanding. It is not necessary that precisely one of the alternative future possibilities be predicted — which is what we often mean by prediction. Now when we understand a person's behavior in terms of his attitudes, goals, perceptions of the situation in which he finds himself, etc. — in short, in terms of the phenomenology of the situation — what we are doing is, so to speak, attaching the facts of the particular case to the terminals of our own response system, i.e., our own personality. We attempt to do this without tying in any of the idiosyncratic characteristics of our own personality to the situation. That is, we try to adjust these boundary conditions so as to exclude certain types of behavior that would be natural for us, and to allow the emergence of types of behavior which we understand very well but which are not characteristic of our particular personality. Some of the boundary conditions are in fact denials of conditions that identify us. But many of the *connections*, the conditional response-sets, carry over; and many of these are far beyond our power to formulate in explicit laws, even if doing so would in itself guarantee understanding. Hence, to the extent that this transfer to another personality is possible — and the extent is very considerable — we are in possession of a useful model for human behavior, namely our own more general human characteristics. For example, although I may not be prepared to put up with flagrant infidelity in my wife, it is not impossible for me to understand the defeated reaction of someone else who decides to condone it in his wife. I understand this because it is a response *tendency* in myself, and with very slight adjustments in the personality parameters I can see that it would be something that I would do myself. I understand this in just the way that I understand the way in which a particular machine works, although it is not one of precisely the same kind as those with which I am familiar. I can see the way in which it is related to the ones with which I am familiar, and the way in which the differences would lead to exactly the differences that I see in its operation.

Combine this procedure of matching the self to another, with the subsequent procedure of observing the (adjusted) self's responses to the environmental stimulus affecting the subject, and we will often get a gestalt response, an insightful recognition of a familiar pattern of behavior, or *verstehen*. Of course, this is a legitimate process and insight, in the same way in which it is legitimate with any other model. It is a complete misconception of the role of model-explanation to suppose that it must be necessary, in the behavioral field, for me to produce precise general laws governing the way in which I and other human beings behave in such situations. It is only necessary that I be able to demonstrate that this is a standard human response, i.e., part of the human repertoire, and that it is not internally incomprehensible. When I have reduced the behavior of the other to this degree of communality with my own, I have properly explained it. And in doing this, the role of *verstehen* is very valuable.

So the *verstehen* theory can be seen as another special in-

stance of scientific explanation through using models. The fact
that the human model happens to be used in explaining human behavior is what makes it special, but it does not make it
unscientific, perhaps even the contrary.

I would like to mention briefly a related line of research. As
we work with computers in the attempt to get them to reproduce
the phenomenon of comprehension in humans, rather than calculation or repetition or recall, for example, we have found that
it becomes necessary to develop the information-handling facili-
ties of the ordinary calculating machine to a very much more
complicated level, involving the capacity for self-perception.
This leads into the antithesis of the anti-*verstehen* approach, the
realization that understanding *requires* us to develop a meta-
level of cognition from which it is possible to use the self as a
model. This research, it seems to me, has led us to considerable
insights into the process of understanding in humans, and also
into the sense in which humans are different from simple calculating machines.

Not only does this account of *verstehen* have some intrinsic
interest, but it follows from it that certain attempts to reform
the teaching of history in order to make historical explanation
scientific are misguided insofar as they attempt to introduce the
requirement of deduction from general laws. I have suggested
above and expounded in detail elsewhere on the alternative
accounts that are legitimate,[2] and which are much more nearly
consistent with the historian's actual activities than the idealistic
account based on this oversimplified conception of physical explanation. It nevertheless quite definitely does follow from what
I see as the correct account that the teaching of history can be
made considerably more "scientific," i.e., the criteria for good
explanations can be exhibited considerably more explicitly, and

---

[2] E.g., in "Truisms as the Grounds for Historical Explanations," in *Theories of History*, ed. P. L. Gardiner (New York: The Free Press, 1959),
pp. 443–475; "New Issues in the Logic of Explanation," in *Philosophy and
History*, ed. Sidney Hook (New York: New York University Press, Spring,
1963); and "Causes, Connections and Conditions in History," in *Philosophical Analysis and History*, ed. William Dray (New York: Harper & Row,
Publishers, 1966), pp. 238–264.

can be used in the evaluation of actual explanations with considerable enlightenment for the student. The same applies to explanations in the other social sciences. So here is another example of a point from the philosophy of the social sciences which comes back to the classroom in the form of specific recommendations about the way in which a substantial social science should be taught.

And there are other aspects of the point that have educational significance. Why is experience the "best teacher"? Because it conditions the basic set of responses involved in understanding or performing until it is reliable, so that the individual does not have to depend on verbal formulations of the connections which (1) are imprecise and incomplete and (2) cannot be transformed into insight without a great deal of practice in application — i.e., without experience. Why are autotelic (play) procedures of considerable power in teaching? Partly, surely, because they convert an available motivation (competition) into a learning motivation, and partly because of the identification and role-switching skills that are part of understanding the opponent's strategy and are themselves examples of behavior-comprehension via *verstehen*-like processes. These answers are simplistic, but I think they do indicate some interesting ramifications of the point discussed above.

Free-Will and Predictability

The issue between determinists as they have commonly conceived themselves and supporters of the doctrine of free will, or libertarians, as they have most commonly been represented, is essentially similar to that between the *verstehen* and "natural-science" theorists about explanation. That is, there is a point of extreme importance being made by both parties, but an eventual reconciliation at a slightly higher level of sophistication is just as demonstrable. This matter is considerably more complex, philosophically speaking, and I can do no more here than briefly outline the kind of solution I have in mind.

A main feature of the libertarian's position has been to maintain that when we feel ourselves to be in the process of making a choice, a choice which will determine our subsequent behavior, we are not under an illusion. This point is absolutely correct. However, it is an error for the libertarian to suppose that this shows that the choice is not determined in the sense of being fully explicable. On the other hand, it is an error for the determinist to suppose that determination of the choice shows that the choice is illusory. The choice is no less crucial than the motion of the sixth gear in a chain of eight gears. Of course, the motion of the sixth gear is determined by that of its predecessors, but it is entirely essential for the transmission of power to the seventh and hence to the eighth gear. If we destroy the process of choice, or interrupt it, we will — in general — alter the outcome behavior. Now the libertarian has often thought that this feeling of the significance of the act of choice shows that the choice is essentially unpredictable. This is in general a mistake, but that it is a mistake does not in the least count against the necessity for the choice, nor against the fact that the choice cannot be predicted with certainty by the man who makes it.

There are certain very peculiar cases which make some qualifications necessary. A fairly interesting special case arises when the predictor, who can in principle predict the behavior of a chooser, reveals his prediction to the chooser in circumstances in which the chooser is strongly motivated to foil the bystander's predictions. In this situation of close feedback we can get an essentially oscillatory situation in which any possibility of a definite prediction by the predictor is ruled out. The situation can be generalized to include the case in which the bystander is not visible and does not reveal what he takes to be the correct prediction, but is in possession of knowledge about the chooser which the chooser knows he has, and from which the chooser is able to deduce consequences about his own (i.e., the chooser's) future choice. If the chooser's motivation is dominantly contrapredictive, then he will still act contrary to any such prediction, which shows that the information possessed by the predictor is either incomplete, or (alternatively) complete but wrong. Of course, a *third* party could be, in principle, predicting the behavior of both the individuals described if the thesis of predictive determinism is correct, but *his* predictions would be falsified if falsifying *them* became important to the predictee. I think that this kind of special case shows that there are limitations to the truth of predictive determinism, even in a classical system; or one could say that the formulation of predictive determinism must be extremely carefully circumscribed. In the general form, in which it is sometimes taken to mean that anyone can in principle predict the behavior of anybody, it is certainly false. We cannot predict the behavior of people who have a certain amount of knowledge about our knowledge about them and who have a certain kind of motivation.[3] This proposition is related in interesting ways to certain other indeterministic claims made about classical physics by Popper and Landé. It is also related to one interpretation of quantum uncertainty, the interpretation which holds quantum uncertainty to be a manifestation of instrumental interference. (I do not believe that interpretation to be a sound one, but it does formulate, albeit in a misleading way, one consequence of quantum uncertainty.)

In most cases, however, predictability in principle cannot be shown to be impossible, a priori. But a priori impossibilities are not the ones that bother us the most. It is perfectly clear that in practice, predictability of most human choices not only is impossible now, but will forever be impossible. This is simply because human choices are determined by a very large number of variables, the crucial values of many of which we cannot obtain, except in a post-mortem examination or in a full-life follow-through, and even in a full-life follow-through we are not — nor will we ever be — in a position to obtain all the data that we need to cover the whole of a person's future behavior. For example, measurements of the extent of the cosmic radiation impinging upon a person's skull from the early pregnancy of his parent until adulthood are very probably required, and it is sim-

---

[3] A fuller discussion of the aberrant case will be found in "An Essential Unpredictability in Human Behavior," in *Scientific Psychology,* ed. Benjamin B. Wolman and Ernest Nagel (New York: Basic Books, Inc., 1965), pp. 411–425.

ply unrealistic to believe that these facts will ever be obtainable without fatal results. And predicting the mutations of his germ-plasm is obviously impracticable, yet they obviously will affect his children, who obviously will affect him in later life. If we were allowed to severely restrict a person's environment, we could probably greatly increase our efficiency of prediction. But this is not the prediction task which we face and are discussing. To rest our claim of predictability upon success with the substitute task would be a form of cheating.

Predictive determinism must be distinguished from explanatory determinism, which is a much more realistic goal. Prediction and explanation are radically different tasks. It is perfectly possible for us to have regularity laws whose truth we have demonstrated — although we do not understand *why* they are true — from which we can predict human behavior, although we cannot explain the behavior. Conversely, it is perfectly possible for us to explain human behavior by demonstrating that it has followed a particular model on a particular occasion, where we could not in advance say which model it would follow. We can do this without involving ourselves in *ad hoc* explanations as long as there is a significant information content in the model that we invoke, in the sense that it does not cover all empirical possibilities. And it so happens that in domains of a very complicated kind, such as human behavior, or the behavior of leaves in the wind, the second type of activity is more easily performed.

Although it is quite true that quantum theory has shown that the truth of determinism is extremely improbable for physical systems, the inevitable consequence of which is that determinism does not hold for human beings, the extent of the error due to quantum uncertainty is so slight as to be normally well below the level of experimental error in a macro-subject such as psychology. But even if its effects were more extensive, quantum uncertainty does not give any sustenance to the doctrine of indeterminism in the sense in which libertarians have maintained it. For there is no reason to believe that its effects coincide with the occasions on which we make choices. In sum, a reconciliation is in order, and we should recognize the importance of the fact that man as a self-studying entity can frustrate predictions in a way in which no other physical entity can, while on the other hand he cannot escape the rule of physical law.

And a computer can perfectly well be built to exhibit deliberate, effective choice and predictive evasiveness as do humans, although it is even more clearly subject to physical determinism, insofar as that principle is true.

Values in the Social Sciences

It is often held that an essential difference between man and the animals is his system of morality, his capacity for producing normative utterances, etc. It is often held, moreover, that this aspect of man's behavior and interests transcends the concern of science. Consequently, it is felt that the social sciences do not provide us with a full picture of man, the valuing creature.

This view is, I believe, completely erroneous, and the reasons which have led people to maintain it should not be dignified by regarding them as embodying an essential truth which can be regarded as part of the whole truth. They embody only a misunderstanding of the truth.

This criticism should only be qualified by the remark that the subject is an extremely difficult one so that it is quite understandable that people might misconstrue the situation. (Indeed, it may well be that *I* have misconstrued the situation!) But as I see it, the situation is that the distinction between facts and values is at best only a distinction between two types of claims made within the domain of rational discourse, supportable by scientific and logical evidence of different kinds, and not a distinction between the concerns of rational empirical inquiry and the concern of man-outside-science. Value-free social sciences are entirely impossible and would be about as useful to the human race as the castration of all males. They are impossible because judgments of the merit of hypotheses, explanations, theories, experimental designs, observations and instruments are value judgments and essential to any science. They are undesirable because the social sciences are the subjects which should solve social problems, and that requires recommendations, not just descriptions. Although value judgments are essential in all science, *moral* value judgments are not essential in the physical sciences. For the second reason mentioned they are highly desirable for most of the applied social sciences. Are they possible? On a modified utilitarian analysis of morality they are perfectly possible, and no other analysis of morality provides the least reason for a rational man to take morality seriously. Hence, the same reason that leads us to adopt a naturalistic conception of truth in the social sciences leads us to adopt a naturalistic conception of morality: it works, and other views do not. The consequences of this view for understanding and teaching the social sciences are, of course, extensive, and I have discussed them elsewhere at some length.[4] The use of discipline in the classroom, the discussion of patriotism and pornography, of democracy and communism, of capitalism and crime are all directly affected.

There are also important connections with the preceding discussions. Moral training requires moral insight, moral motivation requires moral identification (sympathy), and moral responsibility necessitates free will.

CONCLUSION

In the nineteenth century, biology (in the form of evolutionary theory) provided a revolution in man's thought about himself no less profound than the Copernican. The social sciences are now carrying the insights far beyond the still-literary gropings of Freud, to a full and defensible conception of man as a responsible, moral, intelligent super-machine or super-animal and no more. The whole structure of education must be revolutionized in content and in approach in light of this change.

[4] "Student Values as Educational Objectives," in *Proceedings of the 1965 Invitational Conference of the Educational Testing Service* (Princeton, N.J.: Educational Testing Service, 1966); and "Value Claims in the Social Sciences," a monograph of the Social Science Education Consortium, 1966.

Chapter 4 / *The Contribution of Philosophical Anthropology to Educational Development*

THE TASKS BEFORE US

Philosophy in general contributes to educational development by making educational theory self-conscious about its aims and limitations, about its methods and principles of selection, about its presuppositions concerning the nature of man and society and of the human predicament and human development. To stimulate such systematic self-consciousness is the age-old task of philosophizing since Socrates and the venerable Protagoras first exchanged words on whether virtue, like knowledge, was teachable.

How does philosophical anthropology in particular make its contribution to educational development? Unfortunately, the term "philosophical anthropology" has come to be used for many and diverse inquiries. Some use it for a specific branch of anthropology — the world-outlooks of primitive peoples — just as in economic anthropology the economic practices of primitive peoples are studied. Some philosophers take philosophical anthropology to be the systematic critique of the anthropologist's methods of inquiry, such as digging out his metaphysical presuppositions about culture — for example, whether he is a monist in treating each culture as an organic unity or an extreme pluralist in seeing it as an aggregate of isolable and separably replaceable traits. Some philosophers have recently begun to use the term "philosophical anthropology" in a rather unusual way for what has more frequently been called philosophical psychology — an analytic consideration of concepts about man's actions, such as concepts of agent, act, choice, responsibility, and so on. A more traditional use of the term, since Cassirer at any rate, is for that philosophical speculation which seeks a definition of "man" and lines up such candidates as man the tool-user, man the symbol-maker, and so forth. No doubt all of these inquiries have educational implications. For example, if in the last sense I offered a definition of man as the kind of animal that is capable of asking "What is man?" and instead of answering, questioning the meaning of his question, I would have shifted the "essence" of man and I could look for a consequent shift in the "essence" of education — probably to an objective of sharpening the mind by cultivating criticism. I might then go on to trace far-reaching changes in the junior-high-school curriculum, since that is a time when sensitive youngsters wake up to broader issues. I forego the temptation to trace the effects on the bureaucratic structure of educational administration!

I shall deal with philosophical anthropology in none of the special senses I have indicated, but in a more general way. I mean by it the direct utilization of the materials and modes of inquiry developed in modern anthropological work to achieve the philosophical task of developing systematic self-consciousness — in this case, in educational theory. The resultant picture is pretty familiar by this late date in contemporary thought, at least in abstract terms. First, we are liberated from a narrowing ethnocentrism in which we think of our own ways as the fixed order of nature. Second, we come to expect in every phase of life that there has been and can be a wide range of differences. Third, we see differences not simply as varying items but as shaping up into varied systematic patterns. Fourth, in spite of discovered variety — perhaps even because of it — we are better able to discern what kinds of common or invariant elements, what sort of basic unity, there has been in mankind. Fifth, we come to understand the different ways in which human beings have tried to do similar jobs, and are prompted to develop criteria for effectiveness in doing these jobs. Sixth, as a result of such inquiries, we develop the habit of looking for the relations of particular human ways and practices to the general cultural setting; we anticipate the complexity of differing sub-patterns and the interinfluence of groups with different ways; we become conscious of persistent changes and the deeply socio-historical character of human life. And seventh, we gain a sensitive awareness of the forms of expression that the human spirit has taken, and come to realize its creative character. On the practical side, this means that men are always choosing among possibilities in hammering out their next historical steps. On the intellectual side, it means articulating a comparative approach which not merely gives different results but — and this is increasingly central in philosophy today — restructures the questions asked.

All this adds up to a philosophical view of man, not just a few lively items suggested by anthropology. And I need scarcely add that it is a philosophical inquiry, whether carried on by philosophers, or anthropologists, or educators. In principle, of course, this growth of consciousness need not have required anthropological derivation. It might have come directly from sensitive reflection, by observing small differences and extending them in thought, by studying historical changes in a single culture, and so on. In the ancient world, differences in men's ways were closer at hand. The tremendous growth of Western civilization in its uniform aspects has tended to obscure them. It has been the achievement of modern anthropology to exhibit extreme differences, to furnish a larger variety of patterns, and to render comparison analytic and self-conscious. If all mankind spoke a single language which remained basically unchanged, we might never have conceived of alternative languages. It is much easier to develop a science of linguistics when there are thousands of languages. But this is a necessary, not a sufficient condition for self-consciousness. That there are thousands of religions and thousands of moralities has not yet been sufficiently exploited for theoretical understanding. What about the theory of education?

At the heart of any view of educational development lies some concept of education itself. Our traditional concept has been that of schooling — and a static one at that. Here are the materials to be learned, waiting eternally to be imparted. Here are the (more or less recalcitrant) learners-to-be, and here, the teachers trained in the eternally valid modes of transmission. The input is tearful children torn from the bosom of the family. The plant consists in separate buildings shut off from the community. The machine process is what goes on within those sacred precincts. The output is shining faces in caps and gowns, equipped with skills, character, and knowledge. I leave it to students of the history of education to decide whether this really has been a prevalent concept, or is a man of straw for the convenience of educational philosophers.

The broadened view furnished by anthropological materials poses basic questions for such a concept. In his survey of North American primitive education, Pettitt says,

> . . . in primitive society, which had no school system, we find a fairly complete picture of what a people must do to insure the transmittal of its traditions, beliefs, ideals, and aspirations to the younger generation. Through study of such school-free efforts we may obtain a clearer conception of the manifold ramifications of the process of conditioning children and of safeguarding a culture pattern. With such a conception in mind we are then in a better position to judge whether schools and professional teachers, either in justice to themselves or to the public, should be expected to assume the whole responsibility at so much per month.[1]

Philosophical anthropology utilizes the comparative material to elicit two points in our consciousness of what education is doing. The first is a clarified distinction between *schooling* as a narrower concept and *enculturation* as the wider idea of the total

[1] George A. Pettitt, *Primitive Education in North America*, University of California Publications in American Archaeology and Ethnology, Vol. 43, No. 1 (1946), p. 3.

transmission in one mode or another of the ways of the culture from generation to generation. It involves a discovery of the full range of types of ways transmitted and modes of transmission, and a recognition of the selective character of schooling. And so it poses the question of the principles, explicit or tacit, operative in that selection. The second point, once the full range is before us, is the discovery that schooling itself is always doing much more than we are inclined to credit it with. That we recognize this fact is shown in the familiar adage that the personality of the teacher counts almost as much as his knowledge of the subject; but we narrow the view by saying that some types of personality are better able to transmit the subject than others. A full anthropological treatment of schooling startles us by its findings.

My first task here is to exhibit the contributions of philosophical anthropology on these points. But when this is done, we will have merely the raw material on which a theory of educational development can operate, not the principles of selection for the educational focus of the schools. The second task, therefore, is to consider what light anthropological methods can shed on the functional relations of schooling to culture and society as a whole. The outcome of such inquiry is a consciousness of the unavoidably normative character of educational theory. It is commonly recognized that such theory is normative for educational institutions, but the significant point in an anthropological perspective is the ways in which it is normative for the culture as a whole. Hence, my third task will be to raise the question of the value base of normative social decision in our age, and whether it furnishes grounds for a special or central focus in educational development.

What Does the Learner Learn?

No general reference can do justice to the full range of dimensions that come into view when the narrower concept of schooling is enriched by the anthropological concept of enculturation. We require at least a brief itemization.

What strikes us first about the schools, of course, is content — whether we are examining skills such as reading, writing, and French, or subject-matter such as chemistry, mathematics, or Shakespeare. Often we have trouble distinguishing between a skill and a bit of knowledge, and with Shakespeare we may hedge a bit on what we are teaching as we shift from memorization and plot detail to a sense of language or an exuberant outlook. Few theoretical implications might at first seem to follow from the fact that the content of our curriculum has changed over the centuries, nor from the comparative fact that, say, the Aztec priesthood schools included fasting and self-torture. The basic reason why we often take for granted a changing subject-matter of teaching is itself a cultural acquisition. We have stabilized the ideal of a *growing* body of knowledge, and it is this central phenomenon of modern society which is taken to give substance to schooling.

The schools take it for granted that beyond conveying knowledge and skills they are building character. Anthropological impact on the theory of character and attitude development has been quite far-reaching. The lining up of contrasts is overwhelming: for example, the contrast of Zuni modesty and reserve with Kwakiutl ostentation and arrogance; of the typical, matter-of-course generosity found in many American Indian cultures, with our own dominant self-regard; of the male stoicism of the Plains Indians with the gentle tenderness of the Arapesh males; and so on in almost endless contrasts.[2] These striking differences enter into the very organization of concepts as, for example, a particular Chiga character term will apply both to stealing and to inhospitality as if they were one in essence, just as our own term "shiftless" may fuse "lazy," "dirty," and "poor," even though these characteristics are only empirically related under special social conditions. Even more penetrating is the recognition that not only the content of moral attitudes — which acts rouse feelings of guilt — is culturally variable, but the actual type and

[2] See Ruth Benedict, *Patterns of Culture* (Boston: Houghton Mifflin Company, 1934), and Margaret Mead, *Sex and Temperament in Three Primitive Societies* (New York: William Morrow & Co., Inc., 1935).

quality of "conscience" itself, that is, whether one feels guilty or ashamed or disgusted or some other emotional configuration.[3] Also, the ways of expressing feeling are quite different, as can be seen in the impassivity of the Bali, the emotional outpouring of south Europeans, and the familiar British reserve. There are even widely varying attitudes toward such a physiologically common phenomenon as pain — feeling it typically as simply something to be gotten rid of or primarily as a threat because it is a symptom of something wrong in the body.[4] Many of our assumptions about unavoidable attitudes give way in comparisons: for example, the assumed inevitability of stresses and strains in adolescence, which Margaret Mead challenged in her early *Coming of Age in Samoa*. Or the inevitability of childhood anthropomorphism, which she found absent in the early realism of the Manus child. Or the attitudes toward privacy, which she posed in the striking contrast between the Samoan girl who might say that she slept with a boy but would never tell whether she loved him, and the typical American girl who might openly confess she loved a boy but never tell whether she slept with him![5]

Much of what I have said about character and attitude holds equally for social principles. It has taken a long time to realize that our democratic school system has not merely harbored but actively imparted non-equalitarian attitudes. We still do not realize that we are teaching bureaucratic attitudes through the example of the bureaucratic structure of our large educational system. An anthropological survey of our goings-on cannot miss this.

The subtlety of what we are imparting to the young does not

[3] See Margaret Mead, "Social Change and Cultural Surrogates," *The Journal of Educational Sociology*, Vol. XIV (October, 1940), pp. 92–109; also, Ruth Benedict, *The Chrysanthemum and the Sword* (Boston: Houghton Mifflin Company, 1946).

[4] See Mark Zborowski's contrast of Italian and Jewish patients in "Cultural Components in Responses to Pain," *Journal of Social Issues*, Vol. VIII (1952), pp. 16–30.

[5] Margaret Mead, *Coming of Age in Samoa* (New York: William Morrow & Co., Inc., 1928), and *Growing Up in New Guinea* (New York: William Morrow & Co., Inc., 1930).

end with content and skills, character and attitudes and social principles. Hallowell and Redfield and the Kluckhohns have shown how every culture provides orientations of a basic sort for its individuals — modes of reference for their very selves, orientations to space and time and direction.[6] For example, time sweeps from the unseen back to the visible past in front, for the people of one culture, while in another we march forward into the future ahead. (Think how startled we would be if we were told we had a great future behind us!) One people may feel themselves a part of nature, while another feel themselves outside of nature, not cooperating with it but dominating it. In mechanistic fashion, we think of our bodies as machines with almost replaceable parts; primitive societies more often stress a conception of organic unity of self and world. One society lives in the present, another turns its young, as ours does — and the school embodies this stress — to working for the future, postponing gratification, even robbing the present of its non-future meaning. (Recent study has shown this to be a middle-class pattern, which is one reason why middle-class teachers often quite fail to understand the ways of their lower-class pupils.) Often the school imparts overt attitudes to restraint and control. In recent decades we have talked a great deal about leeway for self-expression. The Ashanti sound much more like our conservative critics of progressive education when they say, "When your child dances badly, tell him saying, 'Your dancing is not good,' and do not say to him '[Little] soul, just dance as you want to.'"[7] Beneath overt attitudes to expressiveness or control lie patterns of cultural character that vary both in the modern and primitive worlds.

[6] A. Irving Hallowell, *Culture and Experience* (Philadelphia: University of Pennsylvania Press, 1955), especially Chapter 4; Robert Redfield, *The Primitive World and Its Transformations* (Ithaca, N.Y.: Cornell University Press, 1953); Clyde Kluckhohn and others, "Values and Value-Orientation in the Theory of Action" in *Toward a General Theory of Action*, ed. Talcott Parsons and Edward A. Shils (Cambridge, Mass.: Harvard University Press, 1951); Florence Kluckhohn and Fred L. Strodbeck, *Variations in Value Orientations* (Evanston, Ill.: Row, Peterson & Company, 1961).

[7] R. S. Rattray, *Ashanti Proverbs*, 344, as quoted in J. S. Slotkin, *Social Anthropology* (New York: The Macmillan Co., 1950), p. 526.

Again, in learning itself, the mode in which one is taught produces a second-order learning, what Bateson has aptly called
"deutero-learning." [8] It is at this point that concepts of method,
of authority, of how to go about things and how to fuse thought
and experience are inculcated. Wylie's description of the mode
of teaching in a French village school is a good example of this:

> In teaching morals, grammar, arithmetic, and science the teacher
> always follows the same method. She first introduces a principle
> or rule that each pupil is supposed to memorize so thoroughly that
> it can be repeated on any occasion without a slightest faltering.
> Then a concrete illustration or problem is presented and studied or
> solved in the light of the principle. More problems or examples
> are given until the children can recognize the abstract principle
> implicit in the concrete circumstances and the set of circumstances
> implicit in the principle. When this relationship is sufficiently es-
> tablished in the minds of the children, the teacher moves on to
> another principle and set of related facts.
> The principle itself is not questioned and is hardly discussed.
> Children are not encouraged to formulate principles independently
> on the basis of an examination of concrete cases. They are given
> the impression that principles exist autonomously. They are al-
> ways there: immutable and constant.[9]

A philosopher reading this will be tempted to interpret it as the
deutero-learning of a Cartesian rationalism. Contrast it with
Anthony Leeds' anthropological description of the way of many
American educators:

> . . . the *process* of learning itself is crucial and content secondary,
> if not actually unimportant, since it will be learned by virtue of
> ingesting the process itself, a process labelled "experiencing" and
> conceptually derived from a systematic distortion of the scrolls writ
> by their culture hero, John Dewey. The neonate is to be put through
> "experiences" about which he subsequently "intellectualizes." This
> process apparently prepares him, intellectually or in "life-adjust-

[8] Gregory Bateson, "Social Planning and the Concept of 'Deutero-Learning,'" Conference on Science, Philosophy, and Religion, New York, 1942.
[9] Laurence Wylie, *Village in the Vaucluse* (New York: Harper & Brothers,
1957), p. 73.

ment," as one of the favourite phrases of American educators goes, for any future exigency in learning.[10]

Space forbids a detailed treatment of other phases here, but I cannot forbear running through their variety. To take the question of who teaches: in primitive societies often the whole community serves as teachers, sometimes specialized priests or elders, while among us teachers are a specially trained group. Yet how much among us that is vocational should be learned on the job? Or what part of the learning is of a kind for which at its earlier levels a neighborhood parental group could be enlisted? Again, who is taught? In early China, Linton reminds us,[11] only nobles attended higher schools, and they learned the six liberal arts of ceremonies, music, architecture, charioteering, mathematics, and writing. The ideal of universal education is so recent that its partial achievement calls for reassessing the whole character of our schools. Are we still teaching a kind of charioteering and ceremonies? Again, what are the contexts of learning? We think primarily of a classroom, and even in considering only the college level, have difficulty in thinking of a library as a learning context rather than a preparation for class — to say nothing of the college breakfast table, where students teach each other some of the things they have been learning in class! Primitive societies exhibit more clearly the parental context, the apprenticeship context, learning on the job, the teaching role of striking ceremonials such as initiation rites, the teaching role of designated relatives such as mother's brother or grandparents. Lining all this up poses more consciously the question of who should teach what, where, rather than dumping every critical learning need onto the schools. (Where *should* a child learn how to drive a car, how to repair an electric switch, how to

[10] Anthony Leeds, "Cultural Factors in Education: India, Brazil, the United States, the Soviet Union: Some Problems of Applied Anthropology," in *Contemporary India*, ed. Baidya Nath Varma (New York: Asia Publishing House, 1964), pp. 291–292.

[11] Ralph Linton, *The Tree of Culture* (New York: Alfred A. Knopf, Inc., 1955), pp. 541–542.

dance, and the facts and norms of sexual life?) And what of the techniques of teaching? Primitive societies use not only talk, but music, folklore, and dance to teach: Driberg points out that animal dances are used to portray the characteristics of animals and how to hunt them,[12] and much teaching is done through myths, folk stories[13] (how late we have come to teaching through comic books!), and dramatized ceremonies such as the Hopi use of kachinas (elaborately masked impersonators of ancestral spirits). In all these comparisons there is implicit the obvious lesson that learning is a multiple business, achievable in many ways, and that specialized modes require analysis and evaluation. Plato knew this; do we require philosophical anthropology to convey the lesson?

And what of the prime issue of sanctions in learning? The coercive aspect is often dominant in our educational systems: how many of us still remember the school principal's flat strap for which we were expected to hold out our hand, bravely if not willingly — itself a learning experience? And the truant officer is still much with us. Pettitt concludes that among primitive societies corporal punishment is rare, not because of the innate kindliness of these people but because it is contrary to developing the type of individual personality they set up as the ideal.[14] He finds ridicule, praise, and reward more common. Yet shame can work in different ways. Consider the aggressive shaming of pupils that Wylie describes in a French village school:

> "What is seven times nine, Marie?"
> "I don't know, Madame."
> "Ah! She doesn't know seven times nine. Everyone in this class knows that. Class, what is seven times nine?"
> The class roared the answer.[15]

[12] J. H. Driberg, *At Home with the Savage* (London: Routledge & Kegan Paul, 1932), p. 242.

[13] Walter Goldschmidt points out that educational requirements may be seen to influence primitive folk-tales in the fact that juveniles are utilized as leading characters. See his *Exploring the Ways of Mankind* (New York: Holt, Rinehart & Winston, Inc., 1960), p. 217.

[14] George A. Pettitt, *op. cit.*, p. 161.

[15] Laurence Wylie, *op. cit.*, pp. 84–85.

Compare this with the Pueblo school, in which no child will give the answer till everyone has it, for you must not shame anyone! Of course, in the long run, theory recognizes, the sheer desire to learn would be the very best sanction. (St. Augustine, in the first book of his *Confessions*, looking back on his early sin in preferring Virgil to eternal mathematics, says: "No doubt then, that a free curiosity has more force in our learning these things than a frightful enforcement.") Margaret Mead points out that the shift from learning what everyone agrees everyone would *want* to know, to teaching what some think others *should* know is a differentiating mark between most primitive education and modern complex schooling.[16] Whatever the source of such distinction, once there is this complex, separately existing system maintaining compulsory attendance, the problem of incentives and the discrimination between more and less desirable ones is unavoidable for educational theory.

Let these considerations suffice for exhibiting the impact of the wider concept of enculturation on the narrower concept of schooling. Note, however, that the wide range of dimensions and the breadth of different possibilities within each only throws open — it certainly does not solve — the problem of choice in educational theory. One cannot, for example, simply cull a set of attractive attitudes and character-traits, set them into a beautiful mosaic, and hold them up as a shining model for our school system. We should have, instead, to study the psychological, cultural, and historical depth of our own particular character-formation before making recommendations for reconstruction. Anthropology itself quickly passed beyond merely descriptive

[16] Margaret Mead, "Our Educational Emphases in Primitive Perspective," *The American Journal of Sociology*, Vol. XLVIII, No. 6 (May, 1943), p. 634. Mead traces interesting comparisons with religions proselytizing on the assumption of infallible superiority. She also points to causal factors such as possibilities of changing status and education as a mechanism of change, political factors such as maintaining national loyalty through inculcating a system of ideas, and so on. For consideration of a wide variety of learning modes seen in the general framework of cultural communication, see Mead's *Continuities in Cultural Evolution* (New Haven, Conn.: Yale University Press, 1964), Chapters 4–6.

items of difference to a grounding of difference in the needs, problems, cultural patterning, and historical development of the particular peoples studied. A school system, then, once it has emerged as a separate institutional form — similar to the state or a legal system — is not seen as endowed with an "essence" of its own. At most it has a shifting essence. It has crystallized and temporarily stabilized some aims, methods, techniques, and so on, within which and with which it operates. But it remains bound by a thousand ties to the matrix of needs and causes and informal processes of the body from which it emerged. Its existence and its values reflect the fuller matrix on which it rests; its assessment and its policies can never be self-enclosed and divorced from this reference to its functions. And so we turn to our second task — to consider the contributions of philosophical anthropology to our understanding of the functional relations of schooling to culture and society.

What Does Schooling Do in Society?

The concept of function is, of course, a familiar one in anthropological and sociological theory. The study of functions — latent as well as manifest — reveals men's aims, both through discovering intended consequences and noting social reaction to unintended consequences. For example, anthropologists have noted how the women of a community may feel dissatisfied when the village well is replaced by water piped into individual dwellings. Their labor has been eased and their families' health probably improved, but their daily social life has been ruined; they now have to go out of their way to learn the latest gossip. Now in the village in which I spend my summers we go for drinking water to a spring just outside the village. Occasionally I exchange words with a local inhabitant bent on the same errand. But often a number of cars will line up — usually with out-of-state licenses — and each person will wait, shut off in his car, till his turn comes. Obviously the latent functions of the village well have changed since the days of Isaac and Rebecca.

So, too, the manifest functions of Latin have been transformed in our educational systems, and tradition desperately looks for latent functions to support itself against change.

Anthropology obviously was not needed to reveal the fact that men have aims and that their social practices embody them. But precisely because it studied bits of social practice in the context of fuller cultural patterning it was able to stimulate the *systematic* investigation of functions. When this is done in education, it often reveals unexpected aspects and may quite restructure the mode of evaluation. For example, on questions of discipline — to take a psychological function — Plains Indians are horrified by the idea of our striking a child. When they found it necessary to check a very young child's crying to prevent their camp being located by the enemy at night, they dashed water in its face, and conditioning appears to have taken place effectively. But this was necessity, not cruelty. Other people elsewhere — e.g., the Tikopia in Polynesia — may strike a child occasionally in anger, but not in cold retribution.[17] From an outside observer's view, our modes of corporal punishment are clearly seen as aggressive and incompatible with the dignity of the child.

Again, looking to social functions, I am reminded of Thorstein Veblen's analysis of the latent functions of classical education as an embellishment, with a manifest insistence on its lack of utility, but with a consequent enhancement of repute precisely because it constitutes conspicuous waste.[18] At a later time, in some cities at least, the non-vocational character of liberal arts education, especially for girls, obscured the fact that it was largely preparation for teaching as a career. The role of the contemporary edu-

[17] Raymond Firth, *We, the Tikopia* (Boston: Beacon Press, 1963), p. 141. See also the interesting suggestions concerning modes of corporal punishment (e.g., use of the kitchen spoon or of the hairbrush) and parts of the body focused on, in Martha Wolfenstein, "Some Variants in Moral Training of Children," in *The Psychoanalytic Study of the Child,* Vol. V, ed. Ruth S. Eissler, *et al.* (New York: International Universities Press, 1950), pp. 310–328.

[18] Thorstein Veblen, "The Higher Learning as an Expression of the Pecuniary Culture," Chapter XIV in *The Theory of the Leisure Class* (New York: The Macmillan Co., 1908).

cational system in assisting upward social mobility for lower-middle-class groups and for second-generation immigrant groups is well recognized. So too is its provision of a trained personnel for industry and business. Anthropological concern with total patterning sometimes makes it possible to elicit the functional profile of a whole educational system. Leeds[19] suggests, for example, that the Brazilian school system "is thoroughly tied to the class system and is, in fact, latently intended to support and reproduce its present form. Brazilian education is meant to conserve privilege for the privileged, and to create a manipulable lower class for exploitation by the privileged classes." He supports this opinion by reference both to the multiple types of specific schools for different classes, and to the general ideology of the school system.

Functions become self-conscious when they begin to serve as bases for justification or critique. For example, pure research, as long as it has little manifest social function, is justified in the individual terms of the speculative intellect and its intrinsic value, often with theological components. When its social functions become clear, it becomes "basic research" and is integrated within our university educational system. The contemporary social role of social science is currently a matter of wide controversy. We may leave to historians to delineate the changing functions of intellectual theory in the past few centuries — for example, the impact of the dismal economic science or the succession of political philosophies. For an interesting, out-of-the-way functional suggestion, see Michael Oakeshott's treatment of Machiavelli and Locke as furnishing cribs for princes and classes that had not been born to power but came to it in ignorance; this observation is itself cast within a defense of conservatism.[20]

Again, as functions emerge, even out of differences, there is often a growing awareness of common human aims. Take, for instance, such an apparently remote phenomenon as witchcraft, remembering that spells and ceremonials and the use of herbs

[19] Anthony Leeds, *op. cit.*, p. 298.
[20] Michael Oakeshott, *Rationalism in Politics* (New York: Basic Books, 1962), pp. 24–26.

constitute a quite sizable part of some primitive education. Careful comparative analysis soon causes the shedding of any treatment of the subject as meaningless superstition and leads one to look for the functions of medicinal endeavor, psychological assuagement, substitute satisfaction, social techniques of control, especially in interpersonal conflict, and so on.[21] Thus quite different practices may be seen as ways of dealing with aims that are common. This tends to stimulate the development of criteria for more or less effective achievement. It is a strange dialectic of inquiry by which the search for differences, pressing on into the grounding of those differences, becomes a most helpful way of discovering common aims in human life generally, as well as in education.

On the other hand, the study of education in functional relation to the community does not always yield simple harmonious congruence. There is not merely complexity, but also discrepancy, conflict, and change, especially in a period of socio-historical transformation. These phenomena take innumerable forms. There is often a simple contradiction between educational lessons and social practices. (Wylie, listening to a lesson in which French children repeat and learn by heart, "Let us be the friends and protectors of the little birds," observes, "In a region where a favorite dish is roasted little birds, where a husky man boasts of consuming fifty or sixty warblers at a sitting, there is little likelihood that this lesson will have effect." [22]) There is often a gap between the culture developed in the schools and that of the parent generation that is obvious in immigrant groups but present also in subtler form in native-born groups, because of the rapidity of social change. There is the impact of class differences in aim and mode of life, often focusing sharply in the schools; Lloyd Warner points out that school boards are 94 per cent upper-middle class or higher; teachers, 94 per cent middle-class; and students, 60 per cent lower-class and 30 per

[21] For a particular study of this subject, see J. D. Krige, "The Social Function of Witchcraft," *Theoria*, Vol. I (1947), pp. 8–21.

[22] Laurence Wylie, *op. cit.*, p. 65.

cent lower-middle class.[23] And underlying the whole process are the obvious vast changes in technology, industry, economic life, and the social forms of the twentieth century.

The most extreme conflicts arise in cases in which the educational system is set against the dominant culture, not simply against that of a particular immigrant group. Anthropological studies of acculturation in the modern world amply illustrate such processes. Take, for example, the treatment of education in Absolom Vilikazi's recent *Zulu Transformations, A Study of the Dynamics of Social Change*. The conflict is not something that the investigator need take pains to discover: the people themselves are quite conscious of what is going on. Professor Vilikazi points out that the Zulu distinguish socialization (*imfundiso* or *inkuliso*) from education (*imfundo*). The former equips the child with the values, knowledge, and skills of the culture, and is essentially informal. The latter

> . . . is education in the western sense of the word and is designed to pass on to the child book learning and Christianity and all the things that are characteristic of western civilization. Its aim is and always was to civilize or westernize. It is a new form of upbringing for a new world whose value systems are diametrically opposed to those of the traditional Zulu world. It now dominates the life of the child during all the years of childhood and carries its influence over the childhood years into adulthood.[24]

The consequences of the educational system are quite concrete. The child, not the parent, is able to read a letter or count money. The old culture tells the child not to be disrespectful in talking to an old person by looking directly into his face or eyes; the school teaches that to look away is a sign of shiftiness or dishonesty.[25] The old culture stresses family, kinship, tribal group; the school points to individualism and its education, to economic

[23] W. Lloyd Warner, *American Life: Dream and Reality*, rev. ed. (Chicago: University of Chicago Press, 1962), p. 212.

[24] Absolom Vilikazi, *Zulu Transformations* (Pietermaritzburg, South Africa: University of Natal Press, 1962), p. 122.

[25] *Ibid.*, p. 132.

power and independence. And so on over a wide area of conflicts in belief and attitude.

The changed conception of education we have been considering, imposes a clear mandate on a theory of educational development. The properties of schooling — whether aim, process, or outcome — are to be understood as a function of wider social relations. In societies in which there are internal conflicts, diverse, complex sub-patterns, or basic transformations in process, schooling reflects these variations and conflicts, and educational theory inevitably takes sides or proposes fresh paths. Hence, a theory of educational development is committed to a fuller understanding of causality and qualitative dependence, and it involves normative choices. It is in principle based on a theory of desirable social development and desirable cultural configuration. If it is based on anything less, it is either partially blind or unconsciously reactive. It is to this normative aspect that I now turn.

SOCIAL VECTORS AND EDUCATIONAL DIRECTIONS

If it is the task of educational development to chart the course for the schools, then, as I have suggested, the third major contribution of philosophical anthropology is to bring about the realization that the work of educational development is irretrievably normative, not merely for the schools but for the whole culture.

Take so simple and essential an objective as universal literacy. Professor Leeds suggests that mass literacy accompanies large-scale shifts from a primarily agrarian base to a commercial-manufacturing and commercial-industrial base,[2] and that it is also tied to certain dissolutions in social stratification and the appearance of egalitarian ideals. Hence to move toward universal literacy in India, still only 16.6 per cent literate in 1955, is to effect an overwhelming economic and social transformation.

Or take even the theoretical concepts of an educational theory. We often speak of education as transmitting the culture

[20] Anthony Leeds, *op. cit.,* pp. 304–305.

from generation to generation. But why transmit? Why not change? Is there a conservative potential in the very definition of education? In her article on "Our Educational Emphases in Primitive Perspective" Margaret Mead proposes that "instead of attempting to bind and limit the future and to compromise the inhabitants of the next century by a long process of indoctrination which will make them unable to follow any path but that which we have laid down . . . we [should] devise and practice a system of education which sets the future free." [27] The future will set its own goals.

Now even to set forth such an educational ideal is to offer a critique of our culture, a proposal for its reorientation. Yet this proposal is not wholly divorced from our cultural needs and development, for it expresses the ideal of a fully self-reliant, democratic culture under conditions of extremely rapid social change in which the rate of acceleration of change can be anticipated to rise sharply.

Some educators have at times seemed to thrust upon educational theory the burden of total social change — for example, George Counts in his *Dare the School Build a New Social Order?* in the 1930's. On the whole, an analysis of our society and its culture does not support such a prospect. For one thing, it falls too readily into our cultural habit of piling every problem on the schools and then ignoring the problem elsewhere — forgetting even to increase the school budget! In many respects the schools have followed rather than led in social development: they are under strong traditional controls, they respond to social causes and necessities belatedly instead of exercising whatever leadership they may be capable of, and teachers on the whole have themselves tended to be conservative. Beyond this there is always the risk that when the schools rush in to make changes, a foreshortened analysis of aims, geared to some temporary emergency, may create a situation in which havoc results and the structure that creates the problem is reinforced instead of transcended. The clearest case in recent times was the near-sighted national attempt in the 1950's to gear the schools to na-

[27] *The American Journal of Sociology, op. cit.,* p. 639.

tional policy in the cold war, rather than to pursue the long-range goal of global peace.[28]

For its full articulation, a theory of educational development that looks for lights by which to steer its course cannot rest content with merely upholding general ideals, however attractive, any more than it can with merely solidifying even the best traditions of the schools of the past. To take the currently discussed examples, it can turn neither to the concept of the self-development of the individual of progressive education nor the emphasis on basic subject-learning of the traditionalists. If the analysis I have offered is to point the way, nothing less than a full-scale valuational base which recognizes the complexity of schools in the contemporary world and their roots in our developing historical situation can begin to do the job. Such an inquiry falls into two parts. The first is the determination of the basis for judgment, which is a wider task than education alone, since it is fixing the operative value-determinants for a contemporary outlook in all social endeavor. The second is specifically educational, in applying the base in the light of the means and techniques of the schools in the present period. I will offer a few final remarks on each of these tasks.

I have dealt at length elsewhere with what seem to me to be the constituents of a complex valuational base adequate to value-determination in the contemporary world.[29] I mean the types of constituents that enter, for the content is a still further problem. There will be *perennial values,* such as advancing the body of knowledge. There will be *universal needs,* such as health, attitudes that enable one to cope with reality, sound interpersonal relations. There will be *pervasive goals,* such as possessing special skills or having a job or raising a family. There will be the *great instrumentalities* or central necessary conditions for

[28] For a study of the impact of these events on one field of education, see Paul F. Lazarsfeld and Wagner Thielens, Jr., *The Academic Mind: Social Scientists in a Time of Crisis* (Glencoe, Ill.: The Free Press, 1958).

[29] Abraham Edel, *Ethical Judgment: The Use of Science in Ethics* (Glencoe, Ill.: The Free Press, 1955), Chapter 9. For some application to education, see "Education and the Quest for Values," *The Philosophical Forum* (Boston University), Vol. XX (1962–63).

pursuit of the good life in our historical epoch, such as the industrialization of the globe. And finally, there will be *highly critical contingent factors*, such as the need for peace or the removal of racial discrimination. How to distinguish the genuine from the spurious is a vast problem in itself, involving the cooperation of ethics and all the sciences of man. It means doing a job for ethics in full realization of the kinds of lessons I have suggested for education throughout this essay. But with nothing less than this can we show why love without knowledge is blind, or why knowledge without love is empty, or how to distinguish love itself from its inauthentic shadows. And with nothing less will we be able to show what numerous ways there are for fantasy to replace reality in social relations; how to distinguish the kind of automation by which the machine becomes an extension of man from the kind by which man becomes an extension of the machine; why the attempt to remove racial discrimination in America is an authentic ideal, whereas the attempt to achieve racial separation in South Africa is inauthentic; why the attempt to transcend the capitalist-communist conflict by the growth of abundance is authentic, whereas the attempt to stamp out communism all over the globe is inauthentic. And so on. These are long and arduous tasks. There is no royal road to basic ethical judgment or the determination of social policy. I am suggesting that nothing less than a rounded valuational base worked out in concrete depth will do.

The second inquiry focuses on the schools, what they have to work with and what they can become. Here the task is one of appropriate selection from what the first inquiry has established. It involves discriminating emphases within the host of multiple undertakings. Just as there are desirable courses of conduct which one would not dream of turning over to legal enforcement, so there are desirable social practices whose cultivation may have no place in the school. (For example, it has been increasingly recognized that religion has no place in the public schools; we may ask comparably whether patriotism in the traditional sense does not also belong in the family, in civic, political and other such institutions, rather than in the schools.) Again, just as administrative law grew up under the complex social need for regulation in societies having large-scale industry, so all kinds of educational institutions may arise that are not directly connected with the schools. (Already we have research institutes, at one extreme, and technological rehabilitation centers for displaced workers, at the other. And general adult education has woven its way in and out of the schools, as has educational TV and a kind of "do-it-yourself" education through the use of machines.) We are in for an age of educational experiment — in teaching methods, in content-selection, in setting, and in all of the other aspects of learning indicated above. And this is right and proper, for educational development, though centrally geared at present to the schools, must be society-wide in its vision.

These, then, are the theoretical contributions of philosophical anthropology to educational development: (1) the stimulation of a full, systematic consciousness of the culturally specific character of our historically developed school system; (2) the understanding of variety along all relevant dimensions and the view of alternative possibilities; (3) the search for functional relations and underlying aims; (4) the awareness of the normative character of educational policy for the culture as a whole; and (5) the full relation of educational development to a valuational base that fuses knowledge and value in the given age. Stated abstractly, these contributions may sound bare and truistic, but examined concretely, with comparative cultural detail and in philosophical depth, they can revolutionize our thinking and, if applied, transform our schools.

In conclusion, I should like to ask whether there is a central stress for the schools which one might be tempted to suggest. I think there is, if it will not be turned from a general thread into a monistic aim. I offer it separately here, because it would have to be independently established, and disagreement with it would not in any way affect the theoretical conclusions I have presented up to this point.

I suggest that we think in terms of making our schools *bastions of criticism.* I think the implementation of this recommendation will meet a pervasive need in all areas. Concepts are cracking in scientific work, and new ones are being demanded. Traditional media and standards of taste in humanistic fields are being transformed. Political schemata, ideologies, and neat oppositions are breaking down. The mass transformations of life in the past half century are reaching the point where they have burst into consciousness as the central phenomenon of mankind. Repression, however widespread, has shown its hollowness, whether in the communist world or the Western world. In spite of rightist outbursts, there is a wider intellectual recognition of the need for independent thought than there has been since John Stuart Mill wrote his *Liberty* a century ago. The word "conformist" is fast becoming a term of disparagement. Most recently, we have witnessed the upsurge of the younger generation in a movement whose character — despite its turbulence, impatience, and sharp breaks with many established attitudes — is described by responsible observers as profoundly moral. In the field of foreign policy, we are observing the "uprising" of the professors, who are making the unheard-of demand for wedding more accurate knowledge and greater moral sensitivity with our foreign relations. And most basic of all is the changing social position of education itself, from a requisite for sober work and occasional professions to the necessary prerequisite for the actual running of a machine-automated economy.

But in spite of all these objective conditions for rapid changes and all this flaring of consciousness, I do not think the schools will lead the way. There is, however, a fighting chance that, given their new social role, they can be extricated sufficiently from their traditional servitude. If they can become permanent bastions of criticism, with this commitment as a recognized cultural role, this will add genuine substance to our cultural slogan of freedom.

Chapter 5 / *Education and the Ideal of Personality*

PETER A. BERTOCCI

An essay on the ideal of personality belongs in the middle of a treatise on ethics or on the philosophy of education, for it presupposes the answers to other critical questions. Plato's *Republic* remains the classic example of this fact. As Plato saw, without some conception of the dynamics of human nature and society, and of man's possible relation to the structure of the universe, discussion about the ideal of personality and the aims of education is irrelevant to the human situation. And irrelevance to the individual and the social concerns of man in this kind of world is the one mistake that ethics and education must avoid at all costs. What can man become and what ought he to become? These are the magnetic questions in ethics, each pulling relevant data to themselves and each posing new fields of inquiry for the ethicist and the educator. Hence, before turning to the consideration of the ideal of personality, I must consider briefly three preliminary questions related to this search for an ideal, questions to which my own orientation needs to be clear.[1]

Obligation in Human Experience

The first question is, Why ought I to choose one ideal rather than another?

A human being is always partly satisfied and partly dissatis-

---

[1] The actual tracing of the pattern of values in the ideal of personality begins with the third section, "Existence, Health, and Truth Values," on page 101. Some readers may prefer to start there.

fied. Some of his needs or wants are gratified, but he is also "in want"; he is always desiring something else, if no more than a change just for the sake of change. But a man does not simply experience need or desire; he makes judgments about his needs and desires, judgments that are accompanied by feeling some "ought" or "ought not" about their realization. We must not let any specific theory either about the ought or about human wants blind us to or allow us to over-simplify this complex situation in which a human being usually finds himself.

In the simplest terms, we can say that what a man is and what he wants is always challenged by what he feels he ought to be, do, or want. We cannot disregard either what man is, or what man ought to be, and still claim that we are dealing with concrete human beings. In a word, the ought is the ought *of* man and *for* man and not the ought of some dog or some angel; what *man* ought to do can only make claims on what man is and can become. I am about to propose an ideal of personality which all men ought to realize as soon as possible, and I shall try to show that this ideal is rooted in a critical analysis and synthesis of the value-experiences persons have undergone and, as far as we know, can experience, if, as I shall argue, they are to actualize their full potential.

But someone may ask me, Why ought I to realize my full potential, as opposed to a partial potential? What is it about your ideal of personality that ought to have a hold on me? Or, more generally, Why ought I to choose any one ideal in preference to any other?

I reply, Because part of what it means for you to be a person is to experience *obligation* (not compulsion) to choose what *you* think is best. As a human being, I suggest, you do not simply feel wants and desires. When you, at some choice-point, reflect on the presumable choices before you, do you ever say: I ought to choose X rather than Y, if you believe that Y is better than X? It is Y, that choice which seems to you to offer the closest approximation to the best, that immediately calls for your allegiance. If you later change your mind, and think that X and not Y is in fact the closest approximation to the best, you find yourself "oughting" X and no longer "oughting" Y. Indeed, you are asking me to defend what I suggest is the ideal of personality because you are in the grip of some ideal of truth you acknowledge. You believe you *ought* to accept the best theory possible, as you see it; and you do so because you believe you *ought* to think and choose the best you know.

I have discussed the nature of obligation elsewhere at some length.[2] Here, I will simply summarize by saying that oughting does not develop out of some "is," human or divine. Oughting is a kind of experience — imperative experience, not affective-conative, not volitional experience — that human beings undergo along with sensory, conative, reflective, and appreciative experiences. Ought, in other words, is not an adjective intrinsic to some value that is presumably irreducible to desire or want. Again, a value is not obligatory merely because it is the will of God, or the will of my conqueror, or of my society. Ought is not a quality of any value *as* such. It is an abstraction from oughting, a quality of human experience, an activity persons undergo in relation to those experiences which they claim to be better than others (that is, to be "the best" according to some criterion they discover in their experiences of themselves, and with each other, in this kind of a world).

In other words, the "is-ought" issue is "resolved" by locating the imperative (ought) not in some experienc*ed* values or *cognized* value, but in the matrix of personal being. Ough*ting* is a kind of experienc*ing* or activity, along with think*ing*, want*ing*, sens*ing*, will*ing*, appreciat*ing*. It differs from these other activities by being that activity which, irreducible to any of them, "gives" a person the feeling of obligation, or an imperative *Erlebnis*. When expressed in words, that *Erlebnis* is translatable into: I ought to do the best I know (in a choice-situation). Ought attaches to some value, to some preference, because it is

---

[2] See Peter A. Bertocci and Richard M. Millard, *Personality and the Good* (New York: David McKay Co., Inc., 1963), Chapter 9. In this book, which we have called an essay in psycho-ethics, there is more elaborate discussion of what is suggested in this chapter. See also Peter A. Bertocci, "The Moral Structure of the Person," *Review of Metaphysics*, Vol. 14 (March, 1961), pp. 369–388.

judged to be the best by a person who experiences oughting, the imperative to the best. In other words, I find inadequate both the view that oughting is either the derivative of wanting or thinking, and the view that some specific obligation (I ought to be just!) is obligatory simply because it is the introjection of social norms or *vox populi*, or *vox dei*.

Much more, of course, needs to be said to defend such a position, but in this context there emerges a specific answer to the question, Why *ought* I to realize *my full* potential if, for example, I now do not *want* to? The answer is, If you can be convinced or convince yourself that it is best to realize full rather than partial potential, then you will find yourself feeling that *you ought to do so*. Why? Because you are *you*. Because this *is* your response to your own choice-situations. "You ought," is an ought and not a *must;* you are not compelled to do what *you* feel *obligation to* as the best, but you cannot deny (I should argue) that you do feel obligation when you reflectively say, This alternative is better than that. Again, I cannot change your feeling of oughting, but, should I be able to persuade you as to what the best is, I shall find that you too feel obligation to the ideal or to the best in the total situation as we see it. Neither of us may will as we ought, for we are free not to, but this does not change our feeling of ought to the best. Oughting has authority but not power in itself.

One further note may help to confirm this contention that "oughting to the best in a choice-situation" is universal. If you disagree with my ought, that is, this present ought, you do so because you feel that this ought is not the best (toward which you feel obligation); you are choosing in accordance with your felt imperative to the best. We both always fly from one ought to another on the wings of "oughting the best I know." Hence, in answer to the original question, Why ought you, or I, to choose any particular value?, the answer is, because we are the kind of beings that we are, feeling inevitably an imperative to the best as we know it.

The second preliminary question is, Why try to articulate an ideal of personality?

One preliminary comment may help. Although they have not been using these words, many psychologists have, for reasons I need not pursue here, found themselves urging that persons ought to be "integrated," "mature," "healthy," or that they ought to gain insight into themselves, face reality, be creative, be loving, live authentically. But when we ask, Exactly what do these "injunctions" mean — that is, where do we go from here? — we are left high and dry. Or — to take a philosophic moralist by whom I have been much influenced — Immanuel Kant tells us, on good grounds, I think, to treat persons as ends in themselves and never as means only. But what does it mean to respect personality in myself and in others? Surely I cannot do this without guiding myself by some ideal of what a personality ought to become (because it can so become).

The same concern applies to the injunctions of John Dewey which have been so influential in guiding educational philosophy: Be intelligent! Be democratic! I still ask, What kind of a human being am I aiming for when I become intelligent, when I become democratic?

Again, in respected circles of Christian ethics, I am told that the ultimate good is to love God and my neighbor as myself, that I am to go to my neighbor's side. But what do I do when I get there? I must guide myself, must I not, by some ideal of what my neighbor can be and ought to be, as I see him?

To generalize: in so much ethical, psychological, and religious thought we have become so fearful lest we become "casuistic," "moralistic," "impositionistic," that if we ask what I wish to ask, What kind of personalities are we trying to produce?, we are left with generalities that are not, I should say, relevant enough; we are left with "ideals" that actually have guiding power simply because they do presuppose some hidden conception of the ideal person, or at least an idea of the evils we must avoid. Alas, such general injunctions have also left a vacuum that has been filled all too readily by adherence to some socially accepted code when it came to specifics.

There are serious hazards in the way of my journey back to (but not restricted to) the Platonic and Aristotelian search for an ideal of the kind of personalities human beings *ought* to develop, and which can help to guide our thinking about an ideal society. A philosophy of education seems to me ultimately irrelevant without some such goal.

The third preliminary question involves another far-reaching question in philosophy of personality, Can we define human needs in abstraction from value-claims?

A questionable and sometimes unwitting assumption is often made by psychologists of personality, clinical and otherwise. The motivational "givens" of personality are described without reference to the value-experience of persons, on the assumption that knowledge of basic needs and interests should guide our theorizing about the nature of the good for man. In an adequate psycho-ethics, there can be no adequate theory of value that disregards or misconstrues both underlying and important acquired needs or motives of men. The contention here is that if we are to avoid reducing human needs to presumably overarching and over-riding implacable biological needs, or to infantile stages of human life, it is necessary to guide one's analysis of need-structures by keeping value-structures themselves in mind. Furthermore, values cannot be selected or graded in accordance with a theoretical need-theory or motivational theory alone. For how do we know that values are simple derivatives of a need-theory unless we also carefully inspect the *varied dimensions of human value* on their own terms? Values, in other words, are not addenda to a need-theory. On the contrary, values as experienced may provide important guidelines or clues to basic needs. The ends of human life may throw light back on the beginnings. In sum: we can be satisfied with nothing less than a sensitive interrelating of needs to each other, to abilities, and to environmental demands and opportunities.

In considering these three preliminary questions, we are surrounded by many thorny problems. But our orientation may now be clear. An adequate psycho-ethics needs to be aware of both beginnings and fruitions as the operative conception of man itself is further scrutinized. Neither ethics nor a philosophy of personality must be regarded, even unwittingly, as an adjunct either to a materialistic, a naturalistic, or to a theological psychology of personality. Our data must remain the variety of values which human beings experience in their total situation. In a word, since a theory of ethical values and a philosophy of education is a theory of what human beings can and ought to become in the world as they conceive it, we must accept the task of defining our final view of man and of analyzing value-experience on our way to discovering whether any pattern of values constitutes at least the core of an ideal personality.

EVALUATING VALUES

A value is always an experience of a person: "value" is a term used when a person refers to an *experience he wants* ("disvalue," to an experience he does not want). What is valued (or disvalued) is always the experience — the experience of eating a pear, the experience of hearing (experienc*ing*) Bach, the experience of friendliness. "Value" and "disvalue," in other words, refer to some personal undergoing, to some personal *Erlebnis;* no person, no values or disvalues.

The experiencing of value, however, is not the evaluation of the experiencing. When we *evaluate* we are analyzing and relating immediate value-experiences to each other. Furthermore, in human experience we never start in a value-vacuum, from zero value-experience. We do not begin evaluating at some point of reference beyond the experiences themselves. Evaluating finds us already predisposed toward some values and value-patterns. Before we start reflecting about value-experience, before we start purposeful evaluation, our psycho-physiological natures have already been in the business of reaching for, preserving, and avoiding some experiences.

Accordingly, we do not, when we *e*valuate, create the value-experiencings; we ask questions about them from within our experience simply because we find that the value-experiencings have different qualities, that they conflict with each other, or converge with each other. Thus, when we evaluate, we grade value-experiences in relation to each other, not only in terms of

their felt-qualities, or patterns of felt-qualities, but in relation
to their mutual support or non-support of each other. For example, a man may enjoy the quality of Camels-smoking and
the sociality of smoking with other persons. Let us assume, on
the one hand, that he now comes to enjoy the quality of "smoking-
a-cool-cigarette" without decreasing the sociability, although he
still prefers Camels. On the other hand, he finds that he does
not enjoy the image of himself as a chain-smoker, since he abhors
the possibility of cancer. Should another cigarette be marketed
that does not yield the same immediate quality of enjoyment
(for instance, does not taste as good) but preserves health, he
may switch from Camels. Note that his analysis is of actual
experiences and of foreseeable consequences for further immediate experiences of value.

The further point to note here, however, is that grading value-
experiences, or evaluating them, forces the person to move beyond the experiences themselves to equally obstinate facts about
his physiological and psychological nature in relation to what
creates these value-and-disvalue-experiences — in this case, taste,
sociality, the effects of chain-smoking on his health, his cigarette-
addiction, the sacrifice of other values. In other words, the
evaluating of value-experiences takes us rapidly beyond their
immediately "enjoyed" quality to an understanding of the conditions *within* the person and *beyond* him that produce them.
Again, to evaluate is to become aware of the causal relations
that exist (1) among the experiences of man himself and (2)
in man's interaction with his environment.

It may now be clearer why I hinted earlier that theory of
value will force us to raise questions about the nature of man
and of the world, and at the same time reflect on conclusions to
these questions. If there is a pattern of values that we can affirm
as mutually supportive, it will result not only from the fact of
the experienced quality of the values but also from the relations
they have to each other in the context of human experience in
this kind of world.

Thus, a value-pattern is a description of the world *with
man left in it;* it is a consequence of his relating himself in

thought and action to his own nature, and to his total environment. Values and value-patterns are experiences of man; they *relate* him to his world. To say this is not to court relativ*ism* in value-theory, for man's value-patterns are not the product of his whims or desires, but joint-products of his nature (actual and potential) in interaction with the total nurturant environment. Insofar as values are *adjectival* of persons in their interchange with the environment as it comes home to them, values are also statements about a world that challenges, threatens, and nurtures some of man's choices of value-experience more than others. At the same time, it is hazardous to *assume* that one stage in human development is the criterion for all others.

There is no point in arguing this matter further here, for, in the last analysis, anyone who rejects relativ*ism* must sooner or later suggest some universal value, or pattern of values, actually related to man-in-the-world without being relativistic. Hence, I shall proceed directly to outline a core-pattern of values as normative for all human beings, beings who, experiencing "ought to the best," can never disregard their given needs and abilities, who can never neglect the interchange that destroys or fulfills, impedes or supports their value-experiencing. I shall also make certain comments relevant to educational policy.

EXISTENCE, HEALTH, AND TRUTH VALUES

Persons prefer life to death; there would be no problem about the ethics of suicide, murder, or immortality were this not so. Being and staying alive is the necessary but not sufficient condition for all other values. Yet to be alive, to exist, is already to be engaged in enjoying or suffering value-and-disvalue-experiences. Our question, then, is, What values are mutually enhancing and sustaining? For a human being who can be aware of himself, who can remember and plan, the purpose of life, as Socrates said, is not to live, but to live well.

There will probably be no objection to the statement that healthy existence and survival-with-health is to be preferred to mere existence and mere survival. *Physiological health* is existence-value enhanced by qualities that not only increase the likelihood of survival but give vigor and tone to day-by-day existence. If the only choice were between sheer existence and physical health, there would be no problem, for the experience of health is intrinsically preferable to that of physical weakness or illness.

But the outline of the patterning of values begins right here. The necessity of knowing about our bodies, and of the many factors that affect health, makes us immediately aware of the fact that health-values depend upon other values, the pursuit of which may often endanger health itself. These values are truth-values, that is, all the values involved in searching for and discovering the nature of man in his relation to his total environment. We need minimal existence, not full health, to discover truths that will guide us in our desire for more healthy survival. But the healthiest person may be destroyed by his ignorance of some survival-relationship between himself and his world.

I would not waste space with such obvious remarks, were it not that we tend to overlook a very important consequence for explicit educational theory. We often talk as if the most important thing is the health of our children, whether we are discussing their life at home, at school, or elsewhere. Whatever the stress — whether on excellent buildings, proper food and exercise, and schedules for work, play, and rest that build up the body — in our preoccupation with health, we are succumbing to an over-simplified generalization that a strong body is *the* condition for a sound mind. The American standard of living is frequently applauded when the core of the standard seems to be freedom from hunger, or from pain, disease, and discomfort — *as if these were the conditions for, and not in large part the consequences of, the search for and discovery of relevant truths in the environment.* Hence much more attention is concentrated on the number and cost of schools, on comparative salaries of teachers, than on the kind of teachers employed, the educative process, and the other conditions for helping our young people to become sensitive and creative in the search for truth in this world.

Socrates pointed to the actual relation between truth-finding and the achievement of health when he said that the unexamined life is not worth living. Socrates would have agreed, of course, that men have died, and that millions have lived in ill-health, when more knowledge might have saved them. For human beings, clearly, the dependence of both existence and health on the discovery of truth is so great that we might be tempted to claim that, given existence, *the value upon which all other values depend is the discovery of truth.* And, though more argument is needed for adequate defense, this surely forms much of the ground for the contention that the one thing the school at every level must do for human beings is to stimulate the human quest for truth.

Yet Socrates would have defended the search for truth by saying that the actual experience of sensitive knowing, from perception through empirical generalization to abstract reasoning and speculation, has a quality *as* experienced that is preferable to physical health as such. Who prefers to be a healthy idiot, a moron, or an uninformed and dull person to a curious, problem-posing, problem-solving, reflective person? To paraphrase John Stuart Mill, it is better to be Socrates unsatisfied than a healthy person who has no experience of thinking and truth-seeking. In any case, the healthy person will soon need to depend on the person who is not only healthy but aware of truths relevant to protecting health.

We have hardly started in our search for the pattern of the good life. Yet we have already discovered that though value-experiences are different from each other qualitatively, they do not exist in separate compartments but are mutually related or interpenetrating phases in the experience of persons. *To exist as a human being is to seek health and truth both for their own sakes and for each other. And we know this by observing the qualities of the experiences themselves and the causal web within which they exist.* Each supports the other and furthers the other, and each could be used to destroy the possibility of the other, but the realization of one cannot survive without the actualizing of the other. To this extent, then, our knowledge of the pattern of value consists in our being aware of what actually happens and is possible in human experience.

TRUTH-VALUES AND CHARACTER-VALUES

But the moment we note that truth and health are interrelated, we realize that they are also tied to other value-experiences. I have been talking as if existence and a modicum of health were the only conditions for truth-finding, and as if "knowledge is virtue." But neither knowledge nor virtue is forthcoming for persons who are unwilling to discipline themselves. Virtue presupposes knowledge, but knowledge alone certainly is not virtue; rather, it presupposes what may be called "character." *Character* is the willingness to discipline oneself by one's own ideals; in relation to truth-finding, it is the willingness to sacrifice for the ideal of knowledge to which one adheres.

We can immediately see the relevance of character both to health and to truth-values, and, looking ahead, to every other value in the pattern we shall find. For there are obstacles on the path to truth, and the control of appetites that can create illness calls for self-discipline in accordance with such knowledge as we have. One can provide another with free medical aid, one can see to it that food and housing is adequate for him, but one cannot supply another with the self-discipline he needs in order to avail himself of these goods even when they are within his reach. For so many human beings, the problem of health is not the problem of knowledge but the problem of character. Knowledge and health aids are available; what is lacking is what these persons alone can provide if they are not simply to know the truth but act on it. Knowledge by itself does not guarantee other virtues; nor is it likely to come to those without self-discipline.

I have been stressing that the search for truth puts a special premium on character; but other values and virtues (*moral* values) cannot be over-looked, even in passing. One may seek the truth in order to eat or to become healthy; one may eat in order to think; our human experience shows that we must think in order to eat. But it also tells us that often those who pursue

the truth are required to discipline themselves and make sacrifices not only because the discovery of truth requires self-discipline, but because they are living with others who believe they
will be inconvenienced or hurt by new discoveries. Persons
equally concerned about the truth may jealously throw road-
blocks in the way of any one truth-seeker; they may pile scorn
upon him, and they may add to his need to discipline himself by
his own ideal of truth. We often underestimate how much the
freedom of any one scholar or inventor is dependent on the tolerance of others, and especially on the forbearance of equally
learned scholars. Truth-seeking calls for social self-discipline, for
a sense of humor, and deep-rooted humility on the part of both
the truth-finder and of the community in which he lives. In short,
the discovery of truth presupposes sufficient individual freedom
of will on the part of the scholar as he disciplines himself by
ideals of evidence and not by wishes; and it also presupposes
sufficient social and political tolerance to enable him to pursue
that course. At the same time, he who pursues the truth must
be willing to be censured and to be criticized; he cannot proceed unless he has the will to discipline himself within the total
context of social and political freedom.

Once more, we note one of the instances in which value-theory
posits questions about human nature. I can do little more here
than emphasize that the centrality of character in the pattern of
values forces us to ask questions about the conditions in human
nature (such as needs and human freedom) that make character
possible. But *character* as used here seems to be a monolithic
virtue when in fact it is a trend that exists only in the development of virtues. Were we to turn our attention to the structure
of character, we would find, I think, a pattern of virtues related
to the pattern of values I am here proposing.[3]

But here I must restrict myself to underscoring an understandable but nevertheless egregious error of omission in educational
theory at this point — an error stemming in part from a theoretical, psychological climate that has not favored talking about the
will, or the nature of character itself. The error consists in a de-

[3] See Bertocci and Millard, *op. cit.*, Chapters 16 and 17.

emphasis on character (in this sense) in favor of conduct and "behavior." The omission is understandable, for we cannot give, we cannot teach "character" alone to anyone. Self-discipline by nature rests with the individual, in the last analysis. Yet, though we often pay lip-service to "the need for character," have we integrated it into the aims of education? Have we in educational and social practice created the atmosphere or climate in which character can be encouraged without turning into self-flagellation? Granted that in teaching we cannot communicate character — even in ethics classes or social studies — yet have we built an educational community with the need for this ingredient in personality explicitly in mind? Or have we actually assumed that this phase of human development has been based on a mythological account of man and an outworn ethic? Have we gone so far in demanding that we must "make the material interesting," that "we must involve the individual as participant in the learning process," and so forth, that our students have justified their failure to learn what is not "interesting" or what does not immediately involve them? I suspect that we have actually expected them to exert more self-discipline than our theories of volition allowed.

In any case, we can learn from Immanuel Kant at this point, who said, we may recall, "Nothing in the world — indeed nothing even beyond the world — can possibly be conceived which could be called good without qualification except a good will!" Kant saw that the good will is "the indispensable condition of even worthiness to be happy," as well as the condition for the development of other values. And with unerring insight he also saw that the experience of good will, "the summoning of all the means in our power" to do what seems best, "would sparkle like a jewel with its own light as something that had its full worth in itself." [4]

Indeed, I am now not talking about the enjoyment of physical health; nor am I talking about the joys of truth-finding and con-

---

[4] Immanuel Kant, *Foundation of the Metaphysics of Morals,* first section, in *Critique of Practical Reason and Other Writings in Moral Philosophy,* ed. and trans. Lewis White Beck (Chicago: University of Chicago Press, 1949), pp. 55, 56.

templation. I am talking about another phase of human experience that does not exclusively depend upon other values for its existence. As Kant says, even when our good will does not achieve what it wills, we realize that it is better to have hewn to the line than to have yielded to inclination. The character, the will to discipline oneself by one's ideal, is not the complete good or the sole good even for Kant, but it is a good that enriches every other good, and yet, in the final count-down, depends on the individual's own decision to sacrifice whatever need be for the sake of what some existentialists today are calling "authenticity."

In emphasizing character in the pattern of ideals I am saying no less than this: a human being finds an irreducible satisfaction in living not *by* impulse, not *from* impulse or desire, but from his reflective decision about what is worthwhile, including his desires and needs. This experience of "character" in turn helps to define what it can mean to be human. A human being who has little or no character may be biologically healthy; he may live by truths that others have discovered, but he never knows that "peak" experience (to borrow Abraham Maslow's term) of setting and working his own way toward an approved goal, despite hardship, inconvenience, and risk of failure. A person of character has gone beyond being interactive with, and responsive to, his world; he now is responsive-responsible: he is active and not simply reactive; he lives from within his decisions even as the stimuli from the outside world and the alluring appetites make themselves felt in his development.

If this Stoic, Judeo-Christian, and Kantian teaching is at all true, this stress on character as the core of the pattern of human values must make us more sensitive to its development in the total educational program. As I have already hinted, we tend to exclude from our teaching and programs what we cannot put into a program as subject-matter. Much teaching, both in college and in secondary schools, can become a kind of psychological maneuvering of the individual student, a kind of management of learning, so that we develop a model of the person that fits our strategy. But such strategy, and such a thermometer or computer model of the person, neglects the fact that all the learning in the world cannot replace the value experienced by the person who knows that he can manage his own life within limits, that he can take his own risks, that he can accept responsibility for his own becoming and its effect upon others.

If we can do nothing else, we can remember that we are teaching not subject-matter but persons. I, for one, need to keep reminding myself that I am not teaching philosophy; I am teaching persons. I am, I hope, teaching them the ways, the problems, and answers they would do well to be responsive to as they become philosophically responsible. The pattern of values cannot, in the last analysis, be stronger than the value that at once defines each human venture in goodness, enabling the person to overcome obstacles in actualizing values, and yet it can never be completely determined by such achievements. No character, then no zest, no creativity in the ethical life, and in education.

Not for a moment, then, will I take back the contention that character is the moral crucible for the creation of values. But to insist on this is not enough. He who makes character central to the realization of values must insist equally that character unguided by truth makes for fanaticism. Indeed, the de-emphasis upon character in explicit, ethical, and educational reflection is probably due, in part, to the fact that "the road to hell," to paraphrase William James, "is paved by good will." Crisply put, character without other values is blind, and other values without character are threatened with early death if they are born at all. Why?

Truth, Character, and Affiliative Values

Consider what we would have before us if a personality is strong in the values of health, truth, and character, but is very weak in the value of *affiliation*. (I purposely do not say "love," since I reserve the word "love" for a total style of life and not for one type of value.) By *affiliation* I mean the capacity to be responsive to the needs and wants of others, and to enter into non-parasitic, appreciative relationships. Obviously, we are here running close to the ethical problems of justice or altruism. But whatever the final definition and justification for these, all that is initially in mind here is that a human being has a wanted experience, nay, an intrinsically worthwhile experience, when he knows the quality of affiliation in his relation to others. The person who cannot emotionally care about anyone else, who treats other persons as if they were as incapable as things of response to him, who finds that he cannot willingly accept any responsibility for other persons — that person may have physical health, he may be strong-willed, and he may enjoy his lonely search for truth, but he is a poverty-stricken human being.

Here again, if we knew nothing else about the psychology of personality and the nature of persons, we should be justified in asking psychologists and philosophers to keep in mind that persons do intrinsically enjoy experiences of affiliation and that their theories of the person must take full account of the qualitative experience, affiliation. This unique, irreducible quality of fellow-feeling must guide further analysis into the dynamics and ramifications of the personal and social experience.

Here we need only note how deeply interrelated is the value of affiliation with the creation, conservation, and increase of all the other values. Because persons are born dependent for health, growth, and understanding upon adults, their opportunity for character-development is affected by the willingness of other persons to discipline their own wants so that from the beginning the growing person can make his choices with freedom guided by insight. In a broader context, as we have noted, a person's search for truth is impeded by the unwillingness of others to allow the truth-seeker freely to pursue his investigations and then to publicize his conclusions. The quality of conversation, the development of science, art, industry, the family, church, state — these all depend in large degree on the course affiliation takes in the lives of persons. Indeed so many of the values of life are created in, and enhanced by, mutual sharing and enjoyment, that we need not belabor the importance of affiliation.

Yet here again we cannot forget that affiliation, including friendship and romantic love, can become sentimental unless it is dedicated to the realization of other values. The great seduction in the area of romantic love stems from the failure to realize that affection becomes shallow and insipid when it is not invested in pursuits that keep both persons growing. There is all the difference in the world between, "I like you," and "I love you." To be together is to be together not merely in space, not in body alone, but in the creation and mutual enjoyment of other values. And is it not a dominant fact of experience, for all of our frequent blindness to it, that often the profoundest fellowship, creative of new dimensions in a relationship, is born of mutual sacrifice, of loyalty in suffering?

Indeed, none of the creative dimensions of affiliation are possible without the self-discipline we have called character. At the same time, often the greatest social injustice is the product of affiliative tendencies that are not guided by, or disciplined by, truth. In the name of "our" family, "our" community, "our" country, "our" God, hatred and war have been justified. Hell is let loose by persons who will not allow the truth-claims and the value-claims of others to live with their own in a creative compromise. And when narrow affiliation is linked with strong character, but not linked with enough truth, violence to others, and ultimately to self, results. Once more the interpenetration, the patterning, of values is inescapable.

If a person could develop no other values, but could experience health, truth, character, and affiliation, he would already have a personality that could not only resist evil but create further values. Hence I am tempted, having arrived thus far, to say that these are the critical value-centers of personality. If no other realm of value could be added, this hypothesis that a pattern of values can define the ideal of personality would be well on the way to reasonable verification. For this pattern so far expresses both the needs and satisfactions of men in the everyday rounds of life: fulfillment of the need-value, health, is the enduring foundation of economic and individual activity; the need-value, affiliation (and its protection in family and in social and political institutions as well as in the search for truth), would operate in a vacuum apart from economic and social life. Meanwhile, the development of character, as we have realized, is reflected in, and influences, the creation and increase of these values.

Before going on to the next section, let it be noted that I have been keeping one eye on the *experienced quality* of the values themselves, and another on the *interrelation* that exists between values by virtue of the fact that these experiences have their being in and for persons. Hence, these values and their interrelation have been contributing to our knowledge of what human nature can become in the light of a certain psycho-logic of value.

VOCATION AS VALUE-EXPERIENCE

Our growing pattern of values takes on an even deeper dimension as we make an addition that at once reflects and inspires achievements in the realms of health, character, truth, and affiliative values. I have in mind the value of *vocation*. I am not thinking of vocation as a job, that is, in terms of all its instrumental, economic, and affiliative values. The job one has, the work one does "for a living," may well take its place alongside family experience as the arena in which most persons develop their personalities in association with others. But without wishing to dissociate what I am calling the value-experiencing of vocation from the work one does as part of the economic-socio-political structure, the stress *on vocation as value is on the qualitative satisfaction one experiences when his energies and activities are focused on a task that is large enough to express and challenge his own becoming.* A man's work and its value in a community may indeed be his economic and social capital; it may evoke admiration, respect, and praise from others, and thus be a source of many social and economic values. It can, accordingly, support and express the values of health, truth, character, and affiliation.

Yet all of these values will be enhanced, and the individual will experience creativity in a unique way, if he has a sense of vocation in his life. A vocation is the pivot that gives direction to life in terms of the individual's own total abilities and potentialities; and, to indicate interpenetration once more, his sense of vocation will be affected by his capacity to discipline himself in truth and affiliation.

Long ago Plato argued that each man ought to do what he

can do best, that only thus could he be just to himself and to his fellow-men. Plato did not seem to be troubled about whether the distribution of talents, in relation to the actual needs of men in a given environment, would so interlock that the highest good of all would thus be harmoniously assured. We need not assume that such pre-established harmony would be the case, especially in our society, in order for us to take Plato's basic point more seriously in education. Every person must distinguish between "making a living," or having a job by which he will support himself economically, and having a vocation that brings out the best in him. He is very fortunate if vocation and job are consistent with each other. But it will be fatal to his sense of well-being in the long run if he does not, with the help of his schooling, begin to develop insight into the meaning of this distinction for himself.

Educational policy certainly cannot gear itself mainly to preparing persons for the jobs that need to be filled. Although the person must be free to select the job-preparation he wishes, educational policy cannot be content with less than the provision of graded and diversified programs that will help the person to discover his competencies and the areas that bring him high qualitative satisfaction, mainly because he feels that his own unique constellation of wants and abilities are best fulfilled therein. The fact is that too many people who "are making good money" are bored with life; they are mediocre as persons because their lives have lost the direction and deeper focus that a sense of vocation can give. On the other hand, many persons, especially in an economic world in which automation is spreading, will need to find their sense of vocation outside the purely economic sphere. Persons who do not feel fulfillment somewhere in their everyday concerns are likely to develop a spiritual vacuum, or a psychic disease, that cannot be overcome by activities which give temporary, symptomatic relief only. Will the educational program, especially for adults, not need to provide opportunities for fulfillment rather than for preparation? In the last analysis, must not education for personal, vocational fulfillment supplement the concept of education as job preparation?

AESTHETIC VALUES

Here we are already bordering on another realm of values that consists essentially not in "coping with life," but in expressing oneself creatively. I mean, of course, aesthetic values — and recreational values insofar as they involve aesthetic orientation. By *aesthetic value*, I mean the goal-directed experience of expression and appreciation undergone or "enjoyed" for its own sake.

This is the place to re-emphasize that the realms of value are not compartments of life but moments of experience that live together in the complex of personal existence. Even the most utilitarian pursuits can have their aesthetic moments or phases; the moral ventures of life can express and be enhanced by aesthetic meaning ("the good deed done gracefully"). However, though the setting aside of an hour for aesthetic experience is as ridiculous as setting an hour aside for moral experience, or for worship, the fact remains that we find our lives richer because we can "take time out" to appreciate aesthetic performance and to express ourselves artistically.

Once again we note that in any attempt to define aesthetic values we are defining ranges of qualitative experience that the psychologist and philosopher must not neglect in their descriptions and theorizing about the nature of man. The aesthetic component in human experience, the whole range of the arts, invades every nook and cranny of life and lifts them into a perspective that makes their experience more meaningful for the whole of life because of the aesthetic ingredient. The aesthetic experience and the arts are not incidental luxuries that may be added casually to the main course of existence.

For example, imagine a human life that is dead to the experience of song and music, that makes no response to drama and the visual arts, to whom nothing in nature is thrilling, to whom the comic and the tragic, the beautiful, the ugly, and the sublime make no difference, and you have before you a human being who may sense, feel, and even think and be socially responsive

— and yet know no resonance. At the same time, let a person give himself to the disciplines of aesthetic control in every area of life and he will find a kind of growth that cannot be measured in terms of physical, moral, or intellectual strength alone.

Here, we are aware once more of the plurality of value-experiences, on one hand, and, on the other, the network that binds them together in the person. In seeking the pattern of values, I have been scanning human experience for moments and movements that have been found highly satisfying; I have been impressed by the ways in which they express different facets of personal being and, at the same time, create problems of growth and harmony. If I can draw any conclusion at all from this brief outline, it is this: *The problem of life in the area of value-experiences is to learn how to orchestrate the values so that each may contribute to the whole without losing its distinctiveness.*

Before proceeding further, let us look at a diagram that emphasizes the interpenetration of values in the "pattern." It does not illustrate the "symphonic" dynamism now to be stressed.

A Pattern of Values

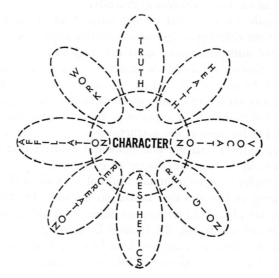

I find the expression "symphony of values" more meaningful than "pattern of values" because it suggests this dynamic development of different motifs or movements which receive attention — but not exclusive attention — from the point of view of the whole. Which orchestration, as each life moves from infancy to old age, and as each life faces the opportunities and exigencies of its existence in physical and social environment, will allow the greatest mutual value-enhancement and support? The death of quality comes if we simply make sure that everything is tasted once, in a cheap democracy of values; at the same time, though specialization in one area of values will be difficult, the ample evidence of such concentrations as intellectualism, aestheticism, and moralism warns us that a life can be warped by the sacrifice of many value-considerations to high hopes of proficiency in one.

Abstractly put, the problem is how to achieve optimum quality without sacrificing variety. Three things are certain: first, tension, conflict, and challenge cannot be avoided in creating, conserving, and increasing values. Second, as is suggested by the notion of symphony, at any one point in the development of a pattern, the problem is to keep the themes of value in a relationship that will be mutually enhancing. Phrases like "nothing too much," "creative counterpoise," "dialectic of values" are different ways of indicating that the human search for quality in value-experience always faces some concrete problem of selection for the sake of ultimate range and unity; risk is integral to the search, and "peace of mind" is inimical to growth.

Concretely put, the problem for any human being in his own life, and for the educator who would help a person to find himself, is to orchestrate value-experience in accordance with that individual's stage of development. Just as every personality is unique, so will the specific ways in which values are realized in a given personality be unique. I am not presenting, as it were, a fixed pattern of personality which becomes a kind of harness to which one fits oneself. Instead, I am suggesting a kind of "mobile" that keeps its inner dynamics, is responsive to its environment, and yet — unlike a mobile or any inanimate object — also creates its responses with the pattern in mind.

I have been showing that the pattern of values is adjectival, is related to the nature of human need, ability, and sensitivity in the nurturant-challenging environment without becoming thereby relativ*istic*. In fact, I would insist that each person, in his stage of growth, in his situation, relate to himself and relate himself to this pattern, not because it is imposed upon him willy-nilly, but because it offers him a regulative guide which grows out of basic human experience, and by which his own pilgrimage in value-experience may be lured. The task of self-education is the task of finding where one is, and how far one can go, in relation to the total human venture in value-realization.

RELIGIOUS VALUES AND PHILOSOPHICAL ORIENTATION

Every dimension of value deserves much more discussion than it has been afforded here, but nowhere do we feel the restriction more than when we seek to place the religious and philosophical dimensions of life. How are the two dimensions related, to each other and to the other dimensions of value-experiencing? The history of the discussion of faith and reason, of home, of church and state, of religious and philosophical education in the schools, tempt one to be silent at this final stage of this discussion. But no ethicist, metaphysician, philosophical theologian, or educational philosopher can in good conscience drop this many-sided problem. For the fundamental issue remains that of being adequately sensitive to the role which each does and can play in a human pattern of values. I can only intimate the approach that seems fair to me.

The seeker — for health, for truth, for creative control (character), for aesthetic expression, for affiliation — inevitably asks whether man is alone in his concern for value-realization. How is man's search for value related to whatever the structure of the world — in itself as it were — is? More specifically, Is there a Being for whom man in his search for values is a value? Historically, these questions have purely theoretical roots as well as purely religious roots. Here I shall confine them largely to the religious.

Whatever the validity of the human religious quest, it would dry up, or cease to be religious, were it not freshened by the continuing experiences, not only of religious "experts" like the mystics in every culture and nation, but also by the testimony of millions who are not religious seers or prophets. At the moment I care not how we finally interpret what I am here calling the experience of the holy. I soberly record the fact that those human beings who have experienced "the holy" have felt that this experience was at least as significant for them in their search for value as any other — indeed they have felt both challenged and supported by it, and it has given them power, they testify, to do what they believe they would not have done otherwise.

Also, human history is simply unintelligible apart from what I am here calling the experience of "the holy." Around it religious creeds and religious communities have been built; much philosophical speculation has stemmed from the attempt to understand and relate this particular human experience to the rest of experience. Often, the inspiring theme for the orchestration of myriad human lives has ultimately depended on a special interpretation of this religious experience.

Let me put this point in another way. Man, in view of his religious experience, has been called a worshipping animal. What he has worshiped has become the source of unity and power in his life — his vocation. The object of worship has fascinated him, gripped him, and claimed his allegiance. In its name he has lived and died; in its name he has been willing to sacrifice all other values; in its name he has been willing to extend himself unrelentingly in the search for truth, beauty, and goodness for himself and others; in its name he has also hurt himself and others.

If such an analysis is at all true, it will be clear that no search for a pattern of values can possibly disregard the experience of the holy and of worship; for it can destroy a symphony of values or it can be its dominating, creative theme. No responsible educator, therefore, can minimize the importance of the search for, or neglect the task of interpreting the meaning of religious experience. Not, at least, if he is interested in the dynamics of the orchestration of values. If at every stage in education there is concern for, appreciation of, and responsibility for both part and whole, then an education that discourages the experience of, and critique of an experience that has such creative and destructive possibilities in a life is simply a halting, truncated education. For education to be unwilling to educate the sense of awe — even as it educates the aesthetic and moral ecstasies — is for education to be willing to neglect the experience that sets the whole of life on fire — for good or evil.

It will be noted that I have not been speaking of religious cults and denominations, which historically have both produced their prophets as well as persecuted and killed them. My concern is more far-reaching, especially in a day when religious and philosophical dogmatism of the right and of the left seem bent on spilling the wine that does not fit their bottles. The school is neither the home nor the church. But a philosophy of education that is a true philosophy of education, and not simply a rationalization for any social, domestic, or religious structure, must keep its attention focused on the dimensions of personality and demand that they be scrutinized with a view to the development of the person as a whole.

The specific problem the philosopher of education faces with regard to religious experience — and which every individual faces with regard to his own religious experience — is a certain authoritarian claim that so readily grows out of the power of the religious experience. This claim is that religious experience (and what is claimed to be revealed in it and delivered through it), be given logical, ethical, and metaphysical priority, or, better, an autonomy which would arrogate other dimensions of experience to it in servile fashion. Yet, whatever one's own final conviction about the validity of a specific religious revelation or interpretation, any person within any religious tradition, must be aware of the differences in the meaning assigned to the religious experience within his tradition. He must face the fact that the quality and meaning or interpretation of religious experience has

varied and, in fact, been affected by its conceived conflict and
harmony with the other facets of life.

For me, the psychologist of personality, Professor Gordon
W. Allport, has expressed the ideal in his description of a mature religious sentiment. Recognizing the need for a unifying
philosophy of life, on the one hand, and, on the other hand,
aware that an immature religious sentiment may keep a personality from growing and promote rigidity, he urges that a mature
religious sentiment, in orienting and committing a person to
*"what he regards as permanent or central in the nature of
things,"* [5] will not dam up the mainstream of personal experience by unstructured ecstasies. Indeed, because it is part of the
individual's search for meaning, the mature religious sentiment
will be more than "just emotional," more than "cold reason"; it
will encourage the person not to allow his life to run off into
little rivulets by confronting him with the demand that he take
seriously the integrity and the possible integration of his values
with an Ultimate Ground of being. The mature religious personality will indeed know that since he cannot know all, he must
remain in uncertainty even as he "learns to act wholeheartedly
even without absolute certainty." [6]

What else have I been pleading for in the above other than
philosophical perspective, both in religious experience and in
every other dimension of life? Obviously a conception of philosophical experiencing is being presupposed — although it has
been partially illustrated in the above. For philosophy means
philosophizing; it is a never-ending search — fraught with the
challenges, the discouragements, and the zest discovered in
every realm of value-experiencing — for connections that are as
ranging and deep as human beings can understand. The person
who is philosophically alive is not necessarily "a philosopher";
he is a person who knows what it is, in his life, at his stage of development, to examine each facet of life for what it is, to see it in
larger context without losing sight of its uniqueness. There is an

---

[5] Gordon W. Allport, *The Individual and His Religion* (New York: The
Macmillan Co., 1950), p. 56.

[6] *Ibid.,* p. 72.

intellectual creativity in such an experience, there is a quality of satisfaction, regardless of the specific outcome of the reflections. What else could have justified Socrates' dictum that the unexamined life is not worth living?

A final note: There can be no symphony of values, no patterning of ideals, for a person who is not willing to be at once attached and detached in his pursuit of values. If one attempts to follow the ideal of personality presented here, the over-riding sin is to pursue one set of values as if it were the end-all and be-all of life. Philosophizing is the attempt to conduct the orchestrating by a score that is created by experimentation with values within a given life, and in human community. Philosophizing does not take the place of living, or of any of the values of living; it is the systematic attempt to connect every fact and value in one's life so that the person will know his connections, and act accordingly.

Chapter 6 / *The Contribution of Philosophy to Educational Development: Summary, Commentary, and Projection*

As I began thinking about this symposium and about my part in it at the conference at Michigan State University on which this volume is based, the memory of one of Lucian's dialogues came recurrently to my mind with some insistence. My faith in my unconscious was strong enough to lead me to reread the piece, *Philosophies for Sale*, which convinced me that Lucian had something to say, at least formally, both to me and to the conference.

The setting of Lucian's dialogue is an auction. Zeus is offering philosophies, ways of life, for sale to men in search of satisfying and useful models for the shaping of their human careers. The dramatic setting is quickly established. Appropriately, it is Zeus who sets the stage:

> Zeus: (*To an attendant*) You arrange the benches and make the place ready for the men that are coming. (*To another attendant*) You bring on the philosophies and put them in line; but first groom them up, so that they will look well and will attract as many as possible. (*To Hermes*) You, Hermes, be crier and call them together.
>
> Hermes: Under the blessing of Heaven, let the buyers now appear at the salesroom. We shall put up for sale philosophies of every type and all manner of creeds; and if anyone is unable to pay cash, he is to name a surety and pay next year.
>
> Zeus: Many are gathering, so we must avoid wasting time and delaying them. Let us begin the sale, then.[1]

[1] *Lucian*, trans. A. M. Harmon (New York: G. P. Putnam's Sons, 1919), Vol. 11, p. 451.

Hermes attempts to auction in succession various philosophies — Pythagorean, Cynic, Cyrenaic, Democritean and Heraclitean — in a combined offering or job lot — Platonistic-Academic, Epicurean, Stoic, Aristotelian and Skeptic. He was unable to sell some philosophies, and the prices bid for others varied from a few obols up to two talents for Socrates. Were my purpose in considering the dialogue a full exploration of the meanings of Lucian's work, I might examine in detail and with pleasure the prices asked and bid, the order in which the philosophies were offered for sale, as well as subtle variations in the responses of buyers to the claims, merits, and demerits of the various philosophies as presented.

But, since my purpose in using Lucian is homiletic, with whatever respect is due to Professor Kaufmann's prejudice against homiletics, I will forego the pleasures of full-bodied criticism here. The question of the Michigan State University conference, "What Can Philosophy Contribute to Educational Development?" is a buyer's question. In fact, it is the same question which, in various forms, Lucian's buyers put to the philosophies which they were considering for possible purchase. And the auction setting which Lucian invoked in his dialogue is, I believe, not inept, analogically, to the setting in which philosophers and the disciplines they represent stand vis-à-vis those now making crucial decisions concerning the forms and directions of educational development — whether these persons or personages are teachers and administrators of schools, colleges, and universities; members of local, state, and national governmental bureaucracies and legislatures; foundation executives; parents; or, increasingly not to be ignored, students. Philosophers as a class now stand, for the most part, outside the arenas of decision encompassed by "educational development," dynamically defined. The deciders have limited continuing communication with philosophers as they shape their judgments and invest their influence in actions in keeping with those judgments. They do at times feel quandaries, dilemmas, and anxieties in the processes of forming, executing, and evaluating plans for and careers in educational development. And they do sometimes feel that they might find clarification and support in their quandaries, dilemmas, and anxieties, if they could find and buy the "right" philosophies and philosophers to assist them. But they are not too sure what "philosophers" have for sale that is relevant to their needs. And, since most philosophers are now external to processes of decision concerning educational development, they, too, are not very clear or confident about the relevance, substantively and methodologically, of their resources to the needs experienced by persons now enacting roles in educational development. Philosophers exhibit varying attitudes concerning the degree and depth of their involvement with these alien persons and processes. In situations in which they wish greater involvement, they feel varying degrees of confusion concerning how they can best "package" and present their relevant resources in seeking, gaining, and justifying the involvement they desire.

Philosophers may wish that the actual relations between philosophers and educational developers were closer than those which characterize the contemporary auction room. We are aware that the very notion of buying a philosophy ready-made does violence to the spirit of philosophy as a disciplined and largely undelegatable quest for clear and valid meanings. A purchased philosophy tends to become a static creed or an otiose public relations display. Yet, in a commercial civilization, the only avenue of educational developers toward a more valid understanding of and respect for the philosophic dimension in their choices may begin with a purchase of philosophic services in projects and programs. If I am not mistaken, a hope for the development of closer and more valid relations between philosophers and educational developers underlay the organization of the conference at Michigan State University. Personally, I wish for closer involvement of philosophers and philosophies in processes of educational development, and I wish further that closer relationships between philosophers and non-philosophers in such processes might take the form of mutual, reciprocal, and continuing collaboration. Some philosophers may wish rather that they were in charge of educational development, legislating its directions and major methodologies. As Professor Kaufmann has reminded us in Chapter 2, Nietzsche thought of the philosopher in the role of legislator, and Plato also craved a ruling role for philosophers in his ideal pedagogical state. Granted the dubious current power position of philosophers in American and world society and education, a vision of philosopher legislators and kings in education seems arrant wish-fulfillment. And, even if it were possible, I, for one, would regard it as undesirable.

My concern for the relations between philosophers, on the one hand, and decision-makers with respect to educational development, on the other, is based on more than my specialized professional commitment to the study of human relations. It stems also from my taking the conference question seriously. What philosophy and philosophers *can* contribute to educational development is a function of the relationships which exist or which may be developed between philosophers and educational developers. The question does not preclude the projection and imaginative rehearsal by philosophers of ideal images of their contributions. In fact, an informed judgment concerning what philosophy can contribute requires an assessment of various projected images of potential and desirable contributions. But the actualization of any image of potentiality depends on the communication between philosophers with now unused visions and intellectual tools and the men and women who make the educational decisions. And the fullness and effectiveness of that communication depends upon the kind and quality of relationships that exist or come to exist between the philosophers and the deciders.

This conviction has influenced the definition I have given to my task of providing a descriptive and critical summary of the conference papers presented here in Chapters 1 through 5. If I may invoke Lucian's dialogue again, I see myself as Hermes, the crier in the processes of an auction. In this intermediary role, I must concern myself with what the buyers — in this case, educational developers — want and need to buy from philosophers, as well as what philosophers believe that they as philosophers have to sell. Before trying to summarize and comment upon the "sales pitches" of our conference philosophers, I will try to "represent" the state of "educational development" in its trend and need.

This will unavoidably involve my own normative and selective diagnosis of the current state and trend of contemporary culture as these now impinge on the development of persons in and out of schools and on the development of educational institutions as well. Perhaps explicitness about my own fallible sense of contemporary educational and cultural need will help others in assessing the adequacy of my own selective and summary comment on the other conference papers.

AMBIGUITIES IN OUR KEY TERMS

There are a number of ambiguities in the meaning of the term "educational development." Clarity about these ambiguities may help both in the communication of my preliminary statement concerning the current state and needs of "educational development" and of "educational developers" and also in the placement of the various conference contributions within the framework of the conference question. There are ambiguities in the term, "philosophy," as well. Some of these will appear later.

In Chapter 2, Professor Kaufmann notes that the "development" we are discussing may refer to the development of individual persons within established processes, programs, and systems of deliberate education. Alternatively, "development" may refer to changes in the institutions of deliberate education. And, though he sees the latter meaning of development focally in changes in educational methods, presumably methods of instruction, this second meaning may be legitimately extended to changes in patterns of administrative control and financial support for education; changes in policies and procedures for the admission, dismissal, and discipline of students, faculty members, and administrators; changes in the organization of the extracurricular life of students and faculty members; changes in the relative emphasis on research and teaching activities in the evaluation of teachers; etc. Professor Kaufmann chooses to focus on "development" as development of the student. And Professors Aiken and Scriven (see Chapters 1 and 3) have accepted the same definitional emphasis.

Professor Kaufmann moves, too quickly as I see it, to conclude that "these two seemingly quite different developments . . . can be viewed as two aspects of the same thing" (page 23). That processes of "educational development" at the institutional and at the personal level are empirically interrelated and intertwined is true. But decisions about development at the two levels tend to be made by quite different people in our society. Teachers and counselors, with varying degrees of participation by students and parents, make most decisions at the level of individual student development. But the leeway these deciders possess, as well as the rewards and support they enjoy, in adapting instruction to fit variations among individual students and groups of students or in bringing instruction into line with their own individual value systems, depends upon decisions made by others at the institutional level. Varying degrees of rigidity in policies with respect to content and procedures, various degrees of commitment to a standard educational product, and various attitudes toward permissible deviation in development among individual students operate in decision-makers and decision-processes at the institutional level of educational development. Actually, decisions concerning the institutions of education and decisions concerning desirable changes in these institutions are often in the hands of persons and groups far removed from the on-going processes of teaching and learning. Governmental executives; legislatures and congresses; lay boards and committees; organized interest groups, including learned and professional societies; school and college administrators; textbook publishers and manufacturers of educational gadgetries; and school and college architects are among those who now influence and/or make decisions about educational development at the institutional level.

The buyers or non-buyers of philosophic competence among decision-makers at these distinguishable levels of educational development are thus quite different people. And philosophic voices, if they are to be heard by these different sets of decision-makers, must speak of and to somewhat different issues — certainly to different confusions, dilemmas, and anxieties. Let me illustrate. Legislation concerning federal grants to education may be oriented to using schools and colleges to redress the imbalance between our production of technically trained scientists and engineers and the comparable educational production of the Soviet Union or of continental China. Or legislation may be oriented toward using schools as more effective vehicles to elevate the social status and employability of Negro children and youth in our economy. And these grants in turn affect the system of rewards, the criteria of evaluation, the status of various sorts of teaching personnel, and the recruitment and training of teachers within our schools and colleges. In making decisions concerning personal development in schools and colleges, teachers, counselors, and students will be constricted by these educational goals, however committed they may be to ideals of rounded and unique personal development, such as those proposed by Professor Bertocci in Chapter 5, or to the notions of supporting individual students in their quest for an examined way of life which several of the symposiasts here represented have expressed. For me, the question is not whether educational programs should serve *either* goals of personal development *or* goals of social development. They must serve both. The thorny problems, in part philosophical, inhere in the reconciliation of these conflicting goals.

Decisions concerning educational development at the institutional level and at the individual level are thus taken today not only by different people who are not in full and free communication with each other; they are also taken on quite different grounds. I tend to share the value orientation of Professors Kaufmann, Aiken, and Bertocci in its stress on the primacy of personal development in educational matters. But I realize that various educational developers are operating today with a quite different hierarchy of educational priorities. Among these, meeting social manpower requirements, as defined by our industrial, military, and scientific elites, and justifying to students policies in service of the national interest and welfare, as officially defined, currently loom large.

Since the two levels of educational development are distinct, though closely interrelated, I believe we must keep them both in mind. Consideration of the needed philosophic contributions to each level is required in any realistic projection or assessment of that contribution.

Another ambiguity in the key terms of the conference stems from a broader and a narrower referent for the word "education." As Professors Edel (see Chapter 4) and Aiken emphasize, "education" may refer to the entire range of the "learned" (as over against biological) development of men and women, often spoken of by anthropologists as "enculturation." Or "education" may be limited to that segment of enculturation encompassed by the word "schooling." Again, I see that adequate assessment of the philosophic contribution to educational development requires a consideration of "education" in both senses, with a priority given today to the broader definition.

The identification of "education" with "schooling" is, in certain contexts of discussion and inquiry, useful and benign. But in the context of defining the range and focus of educational philosophy, the identification seems to me mischievous. If one begins rather by seeing "education" as the enculturation of people into the life of some culture group or another, then the whole range of conflicts, discrepancies, differential emphases, manifest and latent, from one part of a culture to another and from one institutional complex to another, becomes grist to the mill of the educational philosopher. For these conflicts, discrepancies, and differential emphases mark alternatives in "educational" practice as they are communicated to people living and growing up in that culture, whatever the institutional auspices under which the communication occurs, and whether or not the communication occurs in schools or colleges.

The normative analysis and intellectual reconstruction of processes of contemporary enculturation is, then, if I am right, a requirement upon an educational philosophy which would recommend to educational developers concerning the aim and emphasis of their work. If the student of educational philosophy demurs that he is concerned with the analysis and explanation of processes of deliberate and conscious tutelage, not with the dumb, silent and non-conscious aspects of enculturation (his demurral, of course, isolates him from a central issue with respect to the aims of schooling — the relationships between deliberate and non-deliberate enculturation), he must in our day look outside the school as well as inside to locate his subject-matter. For deliberate educational efforts have sprung up, with the growing relaxation of customary and traditional social controls, in various agencies and associations other than schools and colleges and under the aegis of several professions — social work, recreation, health education, nursing, psychiatry, etc., as well as teaching. And discrepant and sometimes incompatible views of "human nature," "maturity," "health," "growth," and "learning" are held and used by these different practitioners. The analysis and adjudication of these conflicting norms and ideals are important parts of the task of the contemporary philosopher of education.

Still another ambiguity in the use of the term "education" has been noted by Professor Aiken. Although he identifies the ambiguity in his discussion of the "teacher," he suggests that it extends to cognate terms. "Education" can be used *descriptively* to signify the various processes, methods, and arrangements employed in a culture to shape, guide, and influence the development of members of that "culture group." By criteria which may be applied in evaluating it, "education" may in this sense be good, bad, or indifferent.

But "education" may also be used in a good sense, denoting only "desirable" processes of schooling or enculturation. Semantic slippage from one usage to another can play havoc with a clear assessment of the effects of "education" in a descriptive sense, and related efforts to redevelop it in a way more in keeping with desirable aims and outcomes. This ambiguity is especially to be guarded against in American culture, where an overinvestment of hope in "education" is highly prevalent. If a little "education" is good — a trivial statement in the normative use of the term but not in the other usage — more "education" may be seen as even better. The effect may be thus to bless current programs and practices indiscriminately. Yet more "education," in its descriptive usage, which leads to undesirable developments in persons and in cultures, is worse than a little such "education."

Semantic slippage from one to another of these uses of "education" can offset and vitiate rational and serious criticism and evaluations of actual processes of schooling and enculturation. And it can also lead to misdirected debates among educators and others concerning the nature of "real" and "true" education rather than possibly fruitful discussions of "better" and "worse" educational efforts.

THE CULTURAL CONTEXT IN WHICH EDUCATIONAL DEVELOPMENT NOW GOES ON

There are several features of contemporary life which inescapably condition efforts to develop and redevelop education in it. These features of contemporary life do not dictate an unequivocal single educational response to our historical situation. On the contrary, they open up alternatives for educational choice and action where once "certainty" as to the right action prevailed in the minds of laymen and educators alike. But although these cultural conditions do not predetermine viable educational responses to them, rational determination of the viability, desirability, and rationality of any and all recommendations and proposals for educational development must take these features of our contemporary situation centrally into account. For this situation is involved in all attempts to answer the question, What must and should modern men learn to do today and tomorrow, and how should they learn to learn? And the viability, desirability, and rationality of philosophic contributions to educational development must be judged by their relevance to these same cultural conditions, whether the intent of the contributior is to bolster or to alter them.

Professor Aiken prefaces his paper with a brief diagnosis of the current human predicament of Western man (Chapter 1, pages 1–7), and Professor Edel offers a diagnosis in his conclusion (Chapter 4, pages 86–91). The following diagnosis is not unlike theirs, though it goes beyond them in some respects.

1. Our culture is marked by pervasive and accelerating changes in human living. Mr. Whitehead has described this

condition in a way that reveals its bearing upon "education" in both its narrow and broad sense:

> Our sociological theories, our political philosophy, our practical maxims of business, our political economy, and our doctrines of education are derived from an unbroken tradition of great thinkers and of practical examples from the age of Plato . . . to the end of the last century. The whole of this tradition is warped by the vicious assumption that each generation will substantially live amid the conditions governing the lives of its fathers and will transmit those conditions to mould with equal force the lives of its children. We are living in the first period of human history for which this assumption is false.[2]

The very notion of education as primarily the transmission of culture rests upon a "vicious" and "false" assumption, in Mr. Whitehead's terms. Yet this notion of education pervades our schools and many processes of enculturation outside the school as well, particularly in the education of children and young people. One alternative is to view education as centrally a process of cultural reconstruction and renewal, to use Professor Brameld's terms. At the level of the individual, the function of education, in this view, becomes the equipping of persons to cope imaginatively, deliberately, inventively, both as individuals and in concert with others, with recurring and expected as well as with unique and unexpected challenges to self and society as established. The philosophic challenge is to project and to assess possible and desirable meanings for this and other viable alternatives in all areas of human life and education.

2. A corollary of the above is the decline of tradition-direction as a valid and dependable guide in human choices and conduct. At the level of the person, this means a decline in the dependability of the "superego" or "conscience" as a personal arbiter of choice and decision.[3] Consensual validation tends to replace dependence upon sanctified traditions, whether external or intern-

---

[2] Alfred North Whitehead, *Adventures of Ideas* (New York: The Macmillan Co., 1933), p. 117.
[3] Allen Wheelis, *The Quest for Identity* (New York: W. W. Norton & Company, Inc., 1958), *passim*.

alized, as a guide to human conduct. But consensual validation as now practiced tends often to become the re-enforcement of special and fragmented orientations to life — specializations abound in the life of knowledge as well as in the life of action — rather than validation against the norms of a "universal" human community that does not now exist, even in idea.

The orientation of human deliberation to a future structured by imaginatively conceived and rationally assessed alternatives — an orientation consistent with the decline of tradition-direction — is hampered in its development by the uncertainties of a future in which the nuclear extinction of mankind is a distinct possibility, if not a probability.

How can education aid persons in their quests for identity and community under these conditions? This is, in part, a philosophic question.

3. Previously segregated cultures are being rapidly desegregated, both across national lines, and across class and racial lines within nations, by the steady encroachment of the mechanical interdependence of men and women. Cultures and subcultures are meeting, clashing, and merging. Men have not yet developed adequate bases for converting desegregation into integration. Processes of "natural" socialization and enculturation now hardly prepare persons who can cope integratively and rationally with the challenges presented by this condition. And deliberate processes of enculturation are stymied by a lack of valid images of trans-national aspiration and valid trans-national criteria for judging the particular norms and ideologies of any culture or sub-culture, including our own.

Northrop has described this condition vividly in its intercultural bearings:

> The East and the West are meeting and merging . . . This is by no means an easy or a perfectly safe undertaking . . . Neither war nor the peacetime problems of our world can be diagnosed as a simple issue between the good and the bad . . . The very number and diversity of conceptions of what the good and the divine is [sic] give the lie to any such diagnosis, and to the ever present proposal that a return to the traditional morality and religion is the

cure for our ills. All that such proposals accomplish is the return of each person, and religious denomination, each political group or nation to its own pet traditional doctrine. And since this doctrine (or the sentiments which it has conditioned) varies at essential points from person to person, group to group, nation to nation, and East to West, this emphasis upon traditional religion and morality generates conflicts and thus intensifies rather than solves our problems. This in fact is the basic paradox of our time: our religion, our morality and our "sound" economic and political theory tend to destroy the state of affairs they aim to achieve.[4]

4. Many of these conditions come to a focus for contemporary men in what Karl Mannheim has described as a "crisis in valuation." He has pointed up the educational bearings of this crisis:

> In the very same social environment we now have the most contradictory philosophies of life. First, there is the religion of love and universal brotherhood, mainly inspired by Christian tradition, as a measuring-rod for our activities. Then there is the philosophy of Enlightenment and Liberalism, with its emphasis on freedom and personality, and its appreciation of wealth, security, happiness, tolerance and philanthropy as the means of achieving them. Then we have the challenge of the Socialists, who rate equality, social justice, basic security and a planned social order as the chief desiderata of the age. But beyond all this we have, as I said before, the most recent philosophy, with the demoniac image of man emphasizing fertility, race, power, and the tribal and military virtues of conquest, discipline and blind obedience.
>
> We are not only divided against each other in our evaluation of the big issues, such as the principle of the Good Life and those of the best social organization, but we have no settled views, especially in our democratic societies, concerning the right patterns of human behavior and conduct. . . .
>
> But the crisis in valuations does not only come to the fore in marginal cases of maladjustment such as crime; we have no agreed educational policy for our normal citizens, since the further we progress the less we know what we are educating for. On the primary levels of education we are undecided whether to aim at creating millions of rationalists who discard custom and tradition and judge each case on its merits, or whether the chief aim of education should be the handing on of that social and national inheritance which is focussed in religion. On the higher levels of education we

[4] F. S. C. Northrop, *The Meeting of East and West* (New York: The Macmillan Co., 1946), selected from pp. 4, 5, and 6. Reprinted by permission.

do not know whether to educate for specialization, which is urgently needed in an industrialized society with a strict division of labour, or whether we should cater for all-round personalities with a philosophical background.

Thus there is nothing in our lives, not even on the level of basic habits such as food, manners, behaviour, about which our views are not at variance. We do not even agree as to whether this great variety of opinions is good or bad, whether the greater conformity of the past or the modern emphasis on choice is to be preferred.[5]

5. Within this confusion and crisis, we have developed a new "establishment" — Don Price's term for the new estate which has been achieved by the sciences, especially by the natural sciences, in all industrialized societies, and particularly in our own.[6] An establishment is a human enterprise granted protection and support by the ruling elites of a society — protection and support which continues through changes and shifts in the leadership of those elites. Industrial elites and governmental elites, civilian and military, have granted to men of scientific knowledge a degree of support and autonomy in their work which is unprecedented in our history.

The problem here is not whether "science" is undeserving or deserving of its establishment. The problem lies rather in the distortions and imbalance which this establishment has introduced into the contemporary life of human learning at all levels. Since an important part of the scientific establishment exists within our institutions of higher education, particularly in our "multiversities," the distortions and imbalances are first felt there in graduate education. Indirectly, they are transmitted downward to other educational institutions — colleges, high schools, and even elementary schools.

The distortions and imbalances are felt in many ways, of which I can only suggest a few here. The emergence of two non-communicating cultures within our life of learning on which C. P. Snow has commented is rooted in this condition. The crises

[5] Karl Mannheim, *Diagnosis of Our Time* (London: Routledge and Kegan Paul, Ltd., and New York: Humanities Press, Inc., 1943), pp. 15–16. Reprinted by permission.

[6] Don K. Price, "The Established Dissenters," *Daedalus*, Vol. 94 (Winter, 1965), pp. 84–116.

in the humanities, which Plumb and his British colleagues have explored recently, are rooted there also.[7] In English universities and secondary schools, the crisis tends to take the form of the threatened disestablishment of the humanities by the new establishment more than in American universities and secondary schools. This is true because, historically, humanistic studies never achieved the status of an establishment in the education of American elites to the degree that they did in English education. In America, the effect of the crisis has been perhaps more to accentuate the semanticists' and epistemologists' errors which Professor Aiken has described in Chapter 1, to hasten the "scientization" of studies in the humanities — in religion, art, and morality. Another response has been to release and foster antirationalistic orientations among "humanistic" teachers and students and among exponents and practitioners of the arts. A closely related effect is to elevate "research" over critical and imaginative "scholarship" and teaching, both in established reward systems for professors and teachers and in the recruitment of distinguished and talented youngsters into learned careers.

Whether or not we see recent "analytic philosophy" as a symptomatic response of academic philosophers to their involvement in this crisis of the humanities, as Ernest Gellner does,[8] we must recognize that academic philosophy and philosophers are deeply affected by this condition. How philosophers choose to respond to it will have much to do with the relevance and significance of the contribution they will be able to make to contemporary educational development.

6. A corollary development to the establishment of science has occurred in the organization of the life of knowledge in our society. The processes of knowledge building, application, and use have widely come to be viewed as an industrial system. And the actual organization of research-utilization chains in many areas of social practice has followed upon this view. The organi-

[7] *Crisis in the Humanities*, ed. J. H. Plumb (Hammondsworth, Eng.: Penguin Books, 1964).
[8] "The Crisis in the Humanities and the Mainstream of Philosophy," in *ibid.*, pp. 45–81.

zation of the knowledge industry has followed principles familiar to students of industrial bureaucracy and of the rationalization of industry. A fundamental division of labor is recognized. In the knowledge industry, the division of labor is among basic research, applied and developmental research, social practice, and consumers and clients of the resources of practitioners. Knowledge-building centers are organized. These are joined by various linkage agents and agencies to centers of applied and developmental research which translate basic research findings into practically applicable methods, devices, and processes — in brief, technologies. In turn, practitioners are educated to utilize and install the technologies developed through applied research in the practice-setting for which they are responsible. Consumers and clients have their needs met better by the knowledge-based technologies which professionalized practitioners make available to them. Or such is the claim and hope of those in command of the knowledge industry. Communication and coordination between different parts of the knowledge industry are accomplished through variously named role occupants in the system — systems engineers, public relations interpreters, managers, and administrators.[9]

The idea of the knowledge industry is not a new one. It was first developed on a large scale within the field of agricultural production through the organization of the land-grant university system and the agricultural extension service. And the planned transformation of American agricultural practices and production which has been accomplished in two and a half generations is evidence concerning the efficiency of the system. The knowledge-industry concept has since been applied in many fields: in medicine, in public health, and, more recently, in education.

I believe this notion fundamentally affects the current cultural definition of "development" in education or in any other area of social practice in which practices of planned change are being

---

[9] See Ronald Havelock and Kenneth D. Benne, "An Exploratory Study of Knowledge Utilization," Boston University Human Relations Center *Research Reports and Technical Notes*, No. 80 (1965), for an analysis of the structure and processes of the knowledge industry.

introduced. Thus "development" comes to mean the processes of translating knowledge acquired through scientific research into technology and the effective installation of this technology in newly institutionalized patterns of practice.

Such technology is designed to meet more effectively some identified and interpreted set of consumer and client needs in a circumscribed area of social practice. Developers look two ways — they scan basic research findings for applicable knowledge. They scan consumer and client populations for unmet or inadequately met needs. Their effort is to invent technologies to connect research knowledge with ways of better meeting these needs.

It is interesting to note that one principal format now being used by the U.S. Office of Education to achieve planned improvements in educational practice is through the establishment of Research and Development Centers in major universities, linked to various cooperating school systems. Linkages are established between basic researchers in the social and behavioral and other sciences; applied and development researchers, who invent and test knowledge-based technologies of teaching and administration; and practitioners (teachers and administrators), who field-test and install these technologies in schools and classrooms to obtain hoped-for improvements in the learning of students — in this case, the customers and clients.

The meaning of "educational development," in this context, centers in the invention and utilization of knowledge-based technologies in the "improvement" of practice. We are also familiar with this meaning for "development" in the familiar classification of "under-developed" and "developed" societies in our discussions and programs of technical assistance to other nations, in our current "war on poverty," conceived as technical assistance to "under-developed" parts of our economy, in urban "redevelopment," etc.

The question of what philosophy can contribute to educational development takes on some new meanings as "development" is redefined in the context of the "knowledge industry" and of "planned change." If I read Professor Scriven correctly, he accepts a definition of education as an applied social science — a view of education quite consistent with the new meaning of "development" which has come with attempts to organize and rationalize processes of knowledge-based social change. He has spoken of the contributions of the philosophy of social science to the education of teachers and students, both methodologically and substantively, when education is seen as an applied social science. He has made a convincing plea for a place for efforts to develop understanding of human behavior in scientific terms in the curricula of schools and colleges. And he has demonstrated how a persistent philosophic quandary — freedom vs. determinism — can be illuminated by the resources of a philosophy of the social sciences. These insights and recommendations give a taste of the important contributions philosophy can make to the intelligence and appreciations required by educators and students as they function in relation to a scientific establishment and with a system of education conceived of as applied social or behavioral science.

Professor Scriven illustrates well the contributions of philosophy to the clarification of the work of researchers, applied researchers, and practitioners in contemporary education. What I find missing in his work is a clear contribution to the clarification of the role of consumer and client within the knowledge industry. How does the consumer or client clarify and represent his needs in processes by which developments designed to "help" him are planned by others more expertly knowledgeable than he? How does he develop his standards of taste as a consumer and as a person, and how does he empower these standards to influence the scientifically oriented practitioners who are serving him in positions of expert authority over him? How can he convert his dependent relationships with functionaries within the knowledge industry to relationships of genuine interdependence in which his autonomy is fostered and maintained?

These are not questions for only a few men and women. They are questions for all of us in our consumer or client role outside the range of our own narrow role of expertise as a producer or purveyor of goods and services (knowledge is one good among others, and teaching one service among other services). All current predictions suggest that the role of all of us as consumers will loom larger and larger in our lives, and our producer role will shrink proportionately in a world of automated production and increased leisure. How can and should our personal investment in a specialized producer role be depotentiated and our investment in a role of tasteful and wise consumption be empowered in education and outside it? This is in part a philosophic question which deserves the attention of philosophers.

I cannot help remembering that educational researchers and developers, when out of role and sometimes when in role, are experiencing the same confusions and quandaries as are other contemporary men. They too are beset by the contemporary crisis in valuation. They too are deprived of tradition-direction and are seeking guidance through processes of consensual validation of value judgments — processes in which "objectivity" is highly problematic, however desirable. They too are beset by the temptations of parochialism in a culturally desegregated and conflicted world. They too are often separated from the resources of the humanities in their primary commitments to the scientific establishment. And they are influencing and in some measure determining the patterns of education for children, young people, and older people, who must learn to cope somehow with these same cultural conditions. Do philosophers have a contribution to make to the clarification of these conditions, to the projection of viable and desirable alternatives for human response to these conditions, and, above all, to the development of adequate methodologies for determining viable and desirable purposes in relation to these conditions? And if they do have a contribution to make to contemporary educational development, how can they best make it?

WHAT THE CONTRIBUTIONS OF PHILOSOPHY CAN BE

Ladies and gentlemen, I, Hermes, have suggested the kinds of quandaries which do and should bring buyers from among the ranks of educational developers to the auction of philosophies.

These are the conditions which bring them when they come to philosophers for help in grounding and clarifying their choices and decisions concerning the education of contemporary men and women, young and old.

It is time now for the philosophers to speak concerning the contributions they believe they can make. I have organized what I have heard them say under five major headings.

1. The Expansion of Consciousness

The most widely affirmed contribution of philosophy to educational development is its contribution to expanded self-awareness, to enlarged consciousness of various dimensions of meaning and value as these affect the beliefs and choices of men, to widened consciousness of alternatives in human conduct and in rationales for human conduct. Socrates' plea for the examined life, for deepened and widened self-understanding, became the plea also of four of our five symposiasts. Our modern identifiers with Socrates, like him, do not see expanded consciousness as an end in itself. They see it as a necessary propaedeutic to the achievement of some moral idea of man as ideally developed — the morally and intellectually responsible bad conscience of his age in Professor Kaufmann; the self-actualizing person of Professor Bertocci; the critical and principled participant-observer in and of life in Professor Edel; or the wise man skilled in the use and appreciation of all modes of human expression, as in Professor Aiken. Fortunately or unfortunately, we have no one among our symposiasts who, like the later Santayana, sees ironic and untrammeled play within the realm of essence as the crown of human life. Yet for all of them, extending sensibility within what Santayana called the realm of essence or meaning is an instrumental, educational goal, if I have not read them wrongly.

Perhaps Professor Kaufmann is closest to the spirit of the historic Socrates in his interpretation and justification of the Socratic plea, although he, like his colleagues, goes far beyond the Socratic *elenchus* in his conception of philosophic method, and, correspondingly, of educational method. He quotes Nietzsche with approval in his identification of the great task of philosophers "in being the bad conscience of their time." The vivisection of the established virtues of a time and place may reveal a new greatness in and for man. Historical and analytic approaches are ways to the revelation of meaning for Professor Kaufmann. But he finds other approaches to the clarification of meaning — sociological and psychological — falling within the possible armamentarium of the philosopher. And he recognizes that the resources of other disciplines — literature, for example — can be taught in a way to expand consciousness. But the type of meaning which he finds more specifically philosophical than any other is the meaning of an action or policy — "its possible and actual consequences and its relation to other actions or policies." And, if I understand Professor Kaufmann correctly, it is in probing the meaning of contemporary, live action and policy issues that the focus of a normative education is to be found. A teacher is not and should not be value-free and presumably he does not expect his students to be or to become value-free either. The normative thrust of education, to which philosophy can contribute, lies in responsible exploration of the ramifications of views on action and policy, both logical and practical, to reveal their meaning and further an assessment of competing views in terms of the considerations, evidence, and arguments that support and that speak against these views. Explorations in meaning are thus in support of a developing discipline on the part of students in rational decisions and actions with respect to life's important issues.

Professor Aiken, too, sees the whole range of meaning as fair game for philosophy and presumably for education as well. He would push explorations of meaning beyond the limits erroneously imposed by the assumptions of semanticism and epistemologism, to coin two ugly words. The limits of "learning about" and "learning that" in education should be sprung to admit emphasis upon "learning how" among the whole range of modes of expression and upon "learning why." In reading his paper, I have not "learned why" Professor Aiken draws the lines of possibility for education short of the "discovery," "invention," and "creation" of new artifacts and meanings. I do not know whether the limitation is set by the nature of man, by the nature of deliberate or formal education, by the competence of "analytic philosophy," which he was called upon to "represent" in the conference, or by some other circumstance.

Professor Bertocci seeks an expansion of consciousness into the various realms of human value-experiencing, in the interest of developing rounded, self-realizing persons who we ourselves ought to aspire to become and to help others to become. The self-orchestration of values, which his ideal person should achieve, involves an orchestration of all possible realms of value-experiencing. For Professor Bertocci, as for Professor Aiken, truth value, while important, is not enough.

Professor Edel is most explicit in finding the central contribution of philosophy to educational development in its stimulation and expansion of self-consciousness among educators, and among students too, as to aims, limitations, methods and assumptions, as well as to the human predicaments which set the educational task in our historical period. He finds important tools for this task in the materials and methods of inquiry which have been developed and are being developed through the efforts of cultural anthropologists. And he illustrates the way in which the application of anthropological modes of inquiry to educational processes and institutions can bring their latent meanings into consciousness to make possible their evaluation and their thoughtful reconstruction when they are evaluated negatively. He finds a role for schools, and presumably for colleges as well, not as leaders in the needed reconstruction of many of our now dysfunctional cultural patterns or in the building of new patterns, but as bastions of criticism of the environing culture. Presumably, students would learn in schools and colleges to become more self-conscious and responsible critics of their culture and of their involvements in it.

I believe that Professor Scriven's notion of the philosophic contribution to educational development includes the expansion of consciousness, although I am not so sure of the priority he assigns to it. He seems, for example, to be seeking grounds for tolerating *verstehen* rather than for embracing it. The use of the methodologies of the social sciences as part of the method of education, conceived of as inquiry, and in the evaluation of educational outcomes, is bound to bring the connections of our actions, both in their antecedents and their consequences, into clearer focus and thus to expand the range of awareness of what we are doing and why we are doing it. And the illumination of philosophic quandaries such as freedom *vs.* determinism and value-fact relationships through the experiences and resources of the social sciences is calculated to have an expansive effect on the awareness of both teachers and students. The educational aim of this expanded consciousness for students, as Professor Scriven sees it, seems to be the ability to think scientifically about human behavior, including their own.

This emphasis upon expansion of consciousness is certainly in line with the need of people in a society cut off from tradition-direction and compelled to find some more self-conscious and planful basis for achieving direction in the conduct of life, both at personal and collective levels of living. The comparative methods for expanding consciousness suggested by Professor Edel also promise, if incorporated into education, to offset the parochialism which results from dependence upon "natural" socialization and enculturation processes other than schooling to shape basic attitudes toward men and cultures and human potentialities — a very widespread dependence in current practice. And Professor Scriven's favored methods of expanding consciousness may also conduce to less parochialism in the products of our education, whether this parochialism centers in nation, social class, or in "race."

2. The Settling of Value Conflicts

No contributor to the conference holds to the cognitive irremediability of value-based conflicts or the rational indeterminacy of value judgments as a fixed doctrine or assumption, as far as I can tell. Yet both extreme relativists and extreme absolutists, whatever their manifest differences, are united by these

assumptions. Relativists and absolutists abound among our educational developers today. And these assumptions do lead to
choices about educational practice which tend to limit it to the
sterile informational focus of "learning about" and "learning that,"
which Professor Aiken deplores, or to open or covert value indoctrination in areas of experience where "sound" doctrine, however
grounded, is thought to need reinforcement, or to some combination of the two. Value *inquiry* is a relatively rare phenomenon in the schools and colleges of America today, as well
as in processes of non-academic enculturation. Yet value inquiry
is what our conference contributors seem to opt for, whatever
their differences. Some educational developers are also concerned to find ways of institutionalizing value inquiry in the
curricula of our schools and colleges. Philosophers do have a
contribution to such a development in education, and this will,
I believe, require some major reconstructions in our educational institutions as well.

Professor Edel emphasizes a responsibility for philosophers to
work along with others in developing a valuational base for
contemporary judgments of value in policy matters and in personal decisions. "Common sense" provides no adequate basis for
such judgment today, whatever some followers of the later
Wittgenstein may believe, because what passes for "common
sense" in various social circles has ceased to be either "common"
or "sensible" in a humanity beset by incessant change, confronted with culturally reinforced value conflicts, and bom-
barded with undigested research knowledge from highly organized and generously supported centers for knowledge-building
and knowledge-utilization. Under these conditions, assumptions
about the cognitive irremediability of value conflicts and the
rational indeterminacy of value judgments are certain to make
sense to many people, educators among them. What Professor
Edel proposes is that philosophers work seriously to construct a
valuational base, compounded of our best knowledge of human
need and potentiality, drawn from our human sciences, our best
knowledge of perennial human aspirations, drawn from the

history of ideas, moralities, and prophecies, as well as from comparative anthropological studies — a valuational base disciplined to the predicaments, dilemmas and choices which our historical situation thrusts upon modern man. I can think of no project that would do more to make education "safe" for probing and responsible value-inquiries than this project which Professor Edel proposes.

3. Refocusing the Method of Rationality

All of our conference contributors seem to believe that the method of rationality needs to be reconceived. All of them believe that philosophizing can contribute to this reconception. And all of them, some with appropriate cautions against methodolatry, seem to agree that discipline in the methods of rationality, properly conceived, is a major outcome to be sought in education, in the functioning of the "products" of education in life outside the schools, and in their continuing self-education.

Professor Bertocci would find a deepened discipline of rationality in ways of orchestrating value experiences, through creative conflict, and in the service of growing self-realization by human beings. Professor Aiken would release education and the thinking of educators and others from the shackles placed upon rationality by the errors of the "semanticists" and "epistemologists." The expansion of meaning and of symbolic adequacy in various modes of expression which he desires are, as I understand him, in the service of a more adequate rationality among men.

Professor Kaufmann proposes a canon of method which he believes applies equally well, with necessary adjustments to differing subject matters, to the rational settling of both factual and normative issues. And he would make a place for the use and learning of such methods in specially constructed forums, if not in most classrooms, in his modestly reconstructed college and university.

Professors Edel and Scriven would incorporate into the methods of rationality — to be employed by teachers and to be employed and learned by students — methods of inquiry and evaluation from cultural anthropology and from other social and psychological sciences.

Reconstructive work on methods of rationality apppropriate to the problems of our time seems to me an important task for philosophers, along with others, in the redevelopment of education both in the broad and in the narrow sense of the word. That the central commitment of self in modern man is properly to methods for its own effective remaking, as John Dewey claimed, would not be affirmed by all of our conference contributors. But I believe they might agree that the acquisition by students of discipline in methods for dealing intelligently with the issues of our time, a discipline acquired through reflective and responsible grappling with these issues, is a major claim upon an education which would avoid moral and social irrelevance, on the one hand, and maladaptive propagation of premature commitment to "solutions" to issues, whether the solutions are traditional or utopian, on the other. The formulation, testing, and communication of such methods is an important contribution to contemporary educational development.

4. The Release and Focusing of Dialogue

Two conference contributors have advocated the release of dialogue among men of knowledge — dialogue addressed to currently central policy and action issues — as an educational good. The release and focusing of normatively oriented dialogue has been a traditional function of philosophers. As I understand Professors Kaufmann and Edel, participation in the critical dialogues they envisage would not be limited to philosophers or students of philosophy. I refer here to Professor Edel's vision of schools, at all levels of formal education, as bastions of criticism of the environing culture in its conflicts and trends. I refer also to Professor Kaufmann's more modest proposal of forums to be developed in higher education as an adjunct to the curriculum. If forums are needed to reduce the normative drought of an education oriented in some large part to the communication of specialized information, I do not see why forums should not be imported also into the curriculum rather than to remain outside. Perhaps the bad conscience of our time needs to be brought to bear upon currently established virtues in the institutions of higher education as well as in institutions outside the university.

5. Projecting Images of Potentiality for Man

At a time when a threatening, clouded future pushes men back to life upon the knife edge of a precarious and conflicted present, men need a future structured with considered and viable alternative images of man and society and their potentialities to guide their choices. And nowhere are viable images of potentiality for man more needed than in processes of educational development. Images of potentiality may come through extrapolating the possibilities for human life implicit in new knowledges of man and his world. They may also arise from envisioned syntheses of values and value orientations now conflicting in man's life of aspiration and action. Or images of potentiality may issue as speculations from a combination of both these sources.

The clearest projection of an image of potentiality for man in our conference papers comes from Professor Bertocci. He has envisioned an ideal self-realizing personality. His vision of personality is disciplined both to scientific knowledge of personality dynamics and to the actualities and potentialities of value-experiencings of various sorts. He develops it through dialectical intercriticism between the virtues and vices of one realm of value experiencing in relation to those of other realms. It is a vision formed to arouse our obligation to realize it more fully. Yet it is a vision open to change in the light of new knowledge of personality and of new analyses of the realms of human value and new accomplishments in these realms. It invites the formulation of alternative images of potentiality for human personality by those who differently interpret and emphasize both its knowledge and its value components. Thus the future becomes clarified and structured for the relevant choices of men, educational developers among them.

I find no comparable projection of images of potentiality for human society and culture among our conference contributions. Professor Aiken specifically states that the good society has no models. Yet he does not hesitate to prescribe "self-knowledge, self-development, self-transcendence, and self-control" as desirable potentialities to be developed in individual personalities. Professor Kaufmann would have the philosopher criticize the imaginative projection of moral and social possibilities which come from venturesome politicians, columnists, and even preachers. But his view of the antithesis between responsible philosophizing and homiletics and rhetoric seems to make it hard for him to see the "philosopher" in a prophetic role. Professor Edel draws back from the committed projection of any "desirable cultural configuration," relying upon criticism of the committed projections of others, non-philosophers presumably, as a central responsibility of schooling. Professor Scriven, committed to psychology as the paradigm science, seems to live in a state of innocence insofar as questions of human organization are concerned.

This objection to the projection of images of potentiality for the reorganization of society by philosophers puzzles me. Why should it be more appropriate for philosophers to project images of potentiality for personality than for society? Certainly, the one projection requires the other if the first is to have any possibility of actualization. For the realization of an ideal of personality depends in some large part upon nurturing and facilitating social and cultural arrangements consonant with the ideal. At the least, an ideal of personality — Professor Bertocci's among others — requires the vision of an ideal school — a social system designed to foster and facilitate the actualization of an ideal in the guided development of flesh-and-blood persons. But as several of our participants have emphasized, personal development depends on processes of enculturation over and above those incorporated in schooling. And this brings us to the projection of institutions and patterns of socialization and enculturation within society consistent with our ideal of personality. The requirement is no different formally, though the content of the projection will be, if we prefer the development of many types of personality rather than the development of one type.

In conclusion, I can only raise questions here about this apparent hesitation by philosophers to project images of potentiality for human society and culture, and venture one suggestion.

1. Is the wariness of contemporary philosophers about the prophetic function of philosophy related to this function's traditional linkage in philosophy with apriorism and dogmatism? Can prophecy not be freed from these dubious linkages and still serve a useful function in the economy of human choice, action, and education?

2. Does the avoidance of projection of images of the good society rest on a perceived lack of any "laboratory" to provide some manner and degree of empirical testing for the projections? If so, could not educational development, both at the institutional and personal levels, and both as schooling and enculturation, provide "laboratories" for such testing? It is in this sense that Dewey once defined philosophy as the general theory of education.

3. Perhaps philosophers feel they do not know enough to venture projections of images of potentiality for society — projections which require substantive knowledge now divided among several, sometimes many, specialists. Perhaps this requires the development of team relationships between philosophers and other men of knowledge in teaching, in basic research, and in applied research, in order to develop the power and confidence to project jointly alternative images of potentiality for persons and for societies — images of potentiality which will populate our clouded future with viable and desirable alternatives and which will help to make possible more rational and seasoned choices about the future development of mankind.

This leads me to invoke again, in conclusion, the image of Lucian's auction room. I, Hermes, believe that the philosophies presented here merit buyers among the educational developers of our time. The buyers need the help philosophers have promised and/or demonstrated. They require continuing collaborative relationships with philosophers to make that help possible. I believe further that there are contributions to educational development that philosophers can make which they have not promised or demonstrated, and which, to some degree, they tend to deny. But these contributions, too, may be forthcoming, if closer collaboration between philosophers and contemporary developers of education can be achieved and maintained. Under the blessing of heaven, let the auction cease.

Index

Absolutists, 143–144
Academic freedom, 41–42
Aeschylus, 27
Aesthetic values, 113–116
Affiliation, 108–111
Agriculture and the knowledge industry, 136
Allport, Gordon W., 119
Ambiguity of terms, 125–130
Ambition, 26
Analytical approach, 27–29
  in education, 29–32
  to meaning, 36–37
Analytical philosophy, 6–7, 32
  a central issue of, 14–16
  development of, 2–4
  Gellner's view of, 135
Anthropology. See Economic anthropology and Philosophical anthropology
Anti-rationalism, 15–16, 135
Appreciation, cultivation of, 5; see also Aesthetic values
Aptitudes, development and testing of, 8, 9, 10
Arapesh, 74
Aristotle, 25
Ashanti, 76
Attitude development, 74–75, 76
Augustine, 80
"Authenticity," 107
Authoritarianism, religious, 118
Automation, 89
Autotelic procedures, 63
Awe, 118
Aztecs, 74

Bateson, Gregory, 77
Behavior, human
  model for, 60–61, 62
  understanding of, 50, 56–63
Berkeley, George, 4
Bildungsroman, 24
Brazil, education in, 83

Cartesian doctrine, 53, 77
Change
  acceleration of, 87, 91
  education as a mechanism of, 80 n., 87
Character, 74–75, 104–108, 109, 110
China, early, education in, 78
Collingwood, R. G., 57
Coming of Age in Samoa (Mead), 75
Common sense, 144
Comprehensibility, 58–59
Computers, 53–54, 62, 67
Confessions (Augustine), 80
Conformity, 41–42, 91
Conscience, 75
Consciousness, expansion of, 140–143; see also Self-consciousness
Consensual validation, 131–132
Conservatism, 83, 87
Consumer role in knowledge industry, 138
Corporal punishment, 79, 82
Counts, George, 87
Courage, 26
Creative expression, 113; see also Aesthetic values
"Crisis in valuation," 133–134
Cultural anthropology. See Philosophical anthropology
Culture(s)
  blending of, 132–133
  as context for education, 130–139

Culture(s) (*cont.*)
   criticism of, 87, 89, 90–91, 142
   role of education in, 81–86
   transmission of, 86–87, 131
      See also Enculturation *and* Society

Dare the School Build a New Social Order? (Counts), 87
Darwin, Charles, 53
Desegregation, 132–133
Determinism, 63, 64–67
"Deutero-learning," 77
Dewey, John, 97, 146, 149
Dialogue, release and focusing of, 146–147
Discipline
   in method, 145, 146
   school, 79, 82
   self, 104, 105, 106, 107, 110, 111
Driberg, J. H., 79

Economic anthropology, 69
Education
   ambiguity of term, 128–130
   as an applied social science, 138
   central question for, 45
   changing social position of, 91
   character as an aim of, 106
   conflicting goals of, 126–127
   conservatism in, 83, 87
   decision-making in, 126
   Dewey's general theory of, 149
   and enculturation, 10–11, 12–16, 131
   experimentation in, 90
   and four cardinal virtues, 26
   importance of social sciences to, 52–68
   inadequacies of, 6
   involvement of philosophers in, 122–124
   liberal, rationalistic conceptions of, 5
   liberal arts, 26–27, 82
   limits on, 20–21, 24, 89
   meaning of, 72

   as a mental process, 9, 10
   normative character of, 73, 86–91, 141
   outside schools, 90 (*see also* Enculturation)
   physical, 9
   relation of, to culture, 81–86
   and religion, 89, 118
   self, 23–24, 116, 145
   as self-development, 12
   social functions of, 82–83
   still not developed as a science, 51–52
   stimulating a self-conscious attitude toward aims in, 69, 70, 71, 140–143
   as transmission of culture, 86–87, 131
   and understanding of human behavior, 50, 56–63
   valuational crisis in, 133–134
   for vocational fulfillment, 112
   what the learner learns, 73–81
   without normative judgments, 29–32, 40–43
      See also Schools, schooling
Educational development
   ambiguity of term, 23, 125–127
   and concept of education, 72–73
   cultural context of, 130–139
   meaning, conditions, and limits of, 7–12, 137–138
   novel of, 24
   suggested contributions of philosophy to, 139–150
   two levels of, 125, 127
Educators, 12; *see also* Teachers
Emotional meaning, 16, 20, 34, 35, 75
Empathy, 57
Enculturation, 10–11, 72–80, 128, 131, 148
   "natural," 132, 143
   teaching and, 12–16
      See also Culture
"Epistemologist's error," 4, 145
Erlebnis, 95, 99
"Establishment," 134–135
Euthyphro (Plato), 2

Evolution theory, 52–53
Existence as a human value, 101–102
Experience
    imperative, 93–99
    learning through, 11
    "peak," 107
    religious, 116–119
    values as, 99, 100, 101, 103, 113
Explanatory determination, 66
Expressions
    creative, 113
    as meaning carriers, 20
    theory of, 3

Facts and values, 39, 40, 42–43, 67
Faculty forums, 43–45, 145, 146–147
Fellow-feeling. See Affiliation
Forums. See Faculty forums
France, educational practices in, 79, 84
Franz Joseph, Emperor, 28
Free will, 63–64, 68
Freud, Sigmund, 68
Functions
    of education in society, 81–86
    self-conscious, 83
    study of, 81–86

Gellner, Ernest, 135
Good life
    great instrumentalities for, 88–89
    images of, 148–149
Good will, 106, 107

Hallowell, A. Irving, 76
Health
    as a human value, 101–102, 103
    psychological, 101–102
    as a universal need, 88
Hesse, Hermann, 24
Historical approach, 27–29, 33, 35–36
Hitler, Adolf, 42
Holy, experience of the, 116–119
    See also Religion

Honesty, 26, 42
Humanities, 5
    disestablishment of, 135
Humbition, 26
Hume, David, 4
Humility, 26

Ideal, choice of, 93–99
Ideal personality, 94, 96–120, 142, 147, 148
Imperative experience, 93–99
Implications, analysis of, 36–37
Indeterminism, 66
India, progress toward universal literacy in, 86
Indians, American, cultures of, 72, 79, 80, 82
Indoctrination of values, 144
Insight, 57–63
Instrumental interference, 65
Instrumentalities for pursuit of the good life, 88–89
Intended meaning, 34–35
Intercultural challenges, 132–133

James, William, 7, 108

Kant, Immanuel, 4, 25, 97, 107
    quoted, 28, 106
Kluckhohn, Clyde and Florence, 76
Know-how, 19–20
Knowledge
    concept of, 18–19
    and love, 89
    as an organized industry, 135–139
    and self-discipline, 104
Kwakiutl, 74

Landé, 65
Language, many types of, 29; see also Linguistic philosophy
Learning
    of attitudes, 74–75, 76
    content of, 73–81
    contexts of, 78, 130–139
    by experience, 11

Learning (*cont.*)
  learners and students, 18
  "learning about," "learning that,"
    "learning how," "learning
    why," 17–21, 141, 144
  second-order, 77
  of skills, 7–8, 9, 19
  See also Teaching
Leeds, Anthony, 86
  quoted, 77–78, 83
Libertarians, 63–64, 66
Linguistic philosophy, 3–4, 7
Linton, Ralph, 78
Literacy, universal, 86
Locke, 3, 83
Logical positivists, 35
Love, 26, 27, 109–110
  and knowledge, 89
Lucian, 121, 122, 124, 149

Machiavelli, Niccolò, 83
Man
  basic aims of, 83–84
  images of potentiality for, 147–
    149 (*see also* Personality, ideal
    of)
  nature of, 52–56, 67, 68, 69, 102,
    105, 113, 146
Mannheim, Karl, quoted, 133–134
Manus culture, 75
Maslow, Abraham, 107
Materialistic approach, 55–56
Maturation, 8, 9
Maturity, 11, 21
Mead, Margaret, 75, 80
  quoted, 87
Meaning(s)
  analytical approach to, 36–37
  assimilation of, 12
  carriers of, 20
  dimensions of, 33–37
  emotional, 16, 20, 34, 35, 75
Method(s)
  a canon of, for examining ideas,
    32–33, 145
  discipline in, 146
  of rationality, 145–146
  study of, 17

Mill, John Stuart, 25, 91
Morality, 4, 67
  naturalistic conception of, 68

Needs
  universal, 83–84, 88
  and values, 98, 110
Nietzsche, Friedrich, 124, 140
  quoted, 25, 28
Non-equalitarian attitudes, 75
Normative judgments, 28–29, 37–
    39, 67–68
  a canon of method applicable to,
    32–33
  in education, 73, 86–91, 141
  education without, 29–32, 40–43
Normative philosophy, 25–26, 36–
    37
  aim of, 39, 45
Normative values, 101–120
  See also Obligation
Northrop, F. S. C., quoted, 132–
    133

Oakeshott, Michael, 83
Obligation, 93–99
"Oughting." *See* Obligation

Parmenides (Plato), 2
"Peak" experience, 107
Peirce, Charles Sanders, 3
Perennial values, 88
Persians, The (Aeschylus), 27
Personality
  ideal of, 94, 96–99, 142, 147, 148
  respect for, 97
  and society, 148
  values to be incorporated in, 99–
    120
Pervasive goals, 88
Pettit, George A., quoted, 72
Philosophers as the "bad conscience
    of their time," 25, 141
Philosophical anthropology, 69–71
  and education, 72–73, 74–75, 77–
    78, 81–82, 90, 142

Philosophies for Sale (Lucian), 121–122
Philosophizing, 69, 119–120
Philosophy
    aims of, 1–2, 7, 25, 69, 70
    rationalistic concepts of, 4, 5
    suggested contributions of, to education, 139–150
    values and, 119–120
        See also Analytical philosophy, Normative philosophy, Personality, ideal of, Philosophical anthropology, Psychology, philosophical, *and* Social sciences
Pitcher, George, quoted, 33–34
Plato, 2, 3, 25, 79, 93, 111–112, 124
Play procedures in teaching, 63
Plumb, J. H., 135
Popper, Karl, 65
Positivists, 33, 35
Predictability, 64–66, 67
Predictive determinism, 64–66
Price, Don K., 134
Protagoras, 69
Psychoanalytical meaning, 34, 35
Psychological meaning, 34
Psychology, philosophical, 70

Quantum uncertainty, 65, 66

Rationalism, errors of, 4–5
Rationality, new concept of method of, 145–146
Recreational values, 113
Redfield, Robert, 76
Relativism, 101, 143–144
Religion
    rationalistic concept of, 4, 5
    and the schools, 89, 118
    and science, 56
    and view of the nature of man, 55–56
Religious values, 116–119
Republic (Plato), 2, 93
Research
    elevation of, 5, 135

in the knowledge industry, 136, 137
    pure and "basic," 83
Research and Development Centers, 137
Russell, Bertrand, 25
Ryle, Gilbert, 7

Samoans, 75
Santayana, George, 140
Schools, schooling
    as bastions of criticism, 90–91, 142, 146
    character and attitude development in, 74–75
    content of, 74–81
    and culture, 87–88
    education as, 128
    and enculturation, 72, 73, 80
    functions of, in society, 81–86
    learning in, 73–81
    limitations on, 20–21, 24, 89
    modes of teaching in, 77–78, 79
    normative nature of, 86–91
    sanctions in, 79–80
    selective nature of, 73
    social principles in, 75, 87, 89
        See also Education, Educational development, Learning, *and* Teaching
Schopenhauer, Arthur, 28
Science
    "establishment" of, 134
    pure philosophy of, 47–48
    and religion, 56
    value-free, 40
        See also Social sciences
Scientific explanation, 58–59, 62–63
Scientific method, contributions of social sciences to, 49–50
Self-consciousness
    expansion of, in educational theory, 69, 70, 71, 140–143
    of functions, 83
Self-development, education as, 12
Self-discipline, 104, 105, 106, 107, 110, 111
Self-education, 23–24, 116, 145

Self-realization, 94, 142, 145, 147
Self-study, 67
"Semanticist's error," 3, 145
Siddhartha (Hesse), 24
Skills, acquisition of, 7–8, 9, 19
Smoking–lung cancer studies, 51
Snow, C. P., 134
Social functions of education, 82–83
Social principles in education, 75, 87, 89
Social sciences
  methodology of, 49–52
  philosophy of, 48–49
  significance of, for education, 52–68, 138
  values in, 67–68
Socialization
  "natural," 132, 143
  Zulu, 85
Society
  good, images of, 148–149
  and ideal of personality, 148
  primitive, 72, 74, 75, 78, 79
  See also Culture
Sociological meaning, 35
Socrates, 2, 14, 25, 30, 31, 37, 69, 101, 103, 120, 140
Spinoza, Baruch, 25
Standard of living, 102
Subsumption under a universal law, 58–59

Teachers, 78
  conservatism of, 87
  decision-making by, 126
  influence of, 24–25
  status of, 16
Teaching
  about the nature of man, 55
  and enculturation, 12–16
  modes of, 77–78, 79
  as only a part of education, 13, 14
  of persons, not subjects, 14
  play procedures in, 63
  rationalistic and anti-rationalistic theories of, 15–16
  and research, 135
  and telling, 14
  See also Learning
Testing, educational, 10
Theology, nature of, 38, 39
Tikopia, 82
Tradition-direction, decline of, 131–132
Truth values, 102, 103, 104–105, 109, 142

U.S. Office of Education, 137
Universal aims and needs, 83–84, 88
Universal literacy, 86

Valuational base, 144–145
Valuational crisis, 133–134
Value inquiry, 144, 145
Values
  aesthetic, 113–116
  affiliation, 108–110
  character, 105–108, 109, 110
  conflicts of, 30, 39, 143–145
  core-pattern of, 101–120
  determination of, 88–89
  discussion of, in faculty forums, 43–45
  evaluation of, 99–101
  existence, 101–102
  as experiences of persons, 99, 100–101, 103, 113
  and facts, 39, 40, 42–43, 67
  health, 101–102, 110
  indoctrination of, 144
  interrelation of, 103, 109, 110, 111, 115
  and philosophy, 119–120
  problem of, in academic context, 5–6
  relation of, to needs, 98, 110
  religious, 116–119
  in the social sciences, 67–68
  truth, 102, 103, 104–105, 109, 142
  vocation, 111–112
  See also Normative judgments
Veblen, Thorstein, 82
Verification, 33–34

Verstehen, 57–63, 143
Vilikazi, Absolom, quoted, 85
Virgil, 21
Vocation, 117
  as value, 111–112

Warner, Lloyd, 84
Weber, Max, 40, 57
White, Morton, 20

Whitehead, Alfred North, 2
  quoted, 131
Wisdom, John, 35
Wittgenstein, Ludwig, 33, 34, 37, 144
Worship, 117
  See also Religion
Wylie, Laurence, quoted, 77, 79, 84

Zulu Transformations (Vilikazi), 85